SO LONG

THE ANTHOLOGY OF POET WARRIORS
VOLUME III

Copyright © 2025 Dead Reckoning Collective, LLC

All rights reserved.
This book or any portion thereof
May not be used or reproduced in any fashion whatsoever
Without the permission of the publisher or the author
Except for the use of quotations

Publisher: Dead Reckoning Collective
Editor: Leo Jenkins & Keith Dow
Book Cover Artwork: Tyler James Carroll & Keith Dow

Printed in the United States of America

ISBN-13: 978-1-963803-10-5 (paperback)
Library of Congress: 2025941378

For more information, please visit:

deadreckoningco.com

Table of Contents

Poetry by Adam Magers 15

Mandala by Tamim Fares 17

Irony by Matthew Sabedra 18

80's in the Rain by Julian P. Seddon 19

wide asleep & sound awake by Julian P. Seddon 20

savages don't suffer by Julian P. Seddon 21

Two Bracelets by John Garman 22

No Combat, No Problems by Jacob Szydzik 23

The Weight of War by Adam Magers 25

Our War by Simon Paul Burke 26

Root Cause by Simon Paul Burke 27

sometimes I go away pt. 3 by Steven Callahan 28

weather forecast on whether war's passed by Steven Callahan 29

this is my story, this is my song by Steven Callahan 30

Perspective by Tom Headle 31

Marines die, it's what we do by Tom Headle 33

PURPOSE by Jake Howell 34

Elegy for Khowst by JS Alexander 35

A Coke and a Smile by JS Alexander 36

Meheranah (Manhood) by JS Alexander 37

RUCKSACK by Chris Madsen 38

Forever War by Mason Rodrigue 39

Easter by Ben Fleming 41

Post Deployment Blues by Mary Garibay 42

fire resistant by Ali Watts 43

Ode to CV by Ali Watts 44

Just Another Day in September by Charles McCaffrey 45

OIF/OEF: A Haiku by Jason Green 46

Solid as a Rock by Jason Green 47

Down into the Dark by William A. Adler 48

The Air was Red by William A. Adler 49

My Nation's Warrior by Martin Lees 50

Sandbags in the Hourglass by Alexander Tirabasso 51

Old Flame, New Fire by Dan Gimm 53

Depths of Bagram by Jacqlyn Cope 54

Legacy by Colin Halloran 55

The Global War on Terror is Over by Don Mateer 56

In my Office by Don Mateer 57

Memories of Sunset in Kandahar by Don Mateer 58

Pain into Purpose by James Kadel 59

OverWatch by Nicole Hughes 60

We Carry Our Brothers with Us by Jason Landau 61

Electric Love by George Briones 62

Vision by Christian Sonnier 63

From Ship to Shore by Harry Foster 65

Midnight Movie Madness by Harry Foster 67

Succeeding by Michael Moriarty 68

Sonnet of the Long Deployment by Michael Moriarty 69

Find Your Meaning by Michael Moriarty 70

All the Kings Men by Paul Hurtt 71

FPS by Jake Hutchinson 72

Conex Boxes & WiFi Hotspots by Lucas Wood 73

The Many Few by Ryan A. Kovacs 74

Things Left Unsaid by Ryan A. Kovacs 75

Estranged Heading by Matt Hayes 76

Looking Back by Matt Hayes 77

Home by Jake Pique 78

Dried Ash by Jake Pique 79

Beginning, Ending by Michael Baumgarten 80

GWOT Fever by Christopher Brown 81

Trending by Benjamin Fortier	82
You Were Just… by Benjamin Fortier	83
Who Did I Kill? By Cokie	84
The Duel by Cokie	85
Christus Rex by Cokie	87
Green Monster by Brooke Bottensek	89
Salty by Olivia A. Garard	90
Five-Star Google Reviews […] by Olivia A. Garard	91
autec by Caleb Durden	92
The Vines by Rodolfo Garcia	93
The Other Side by Lani Hankins	94
(Untitled) by Demere Kasper Hess	95
On Reading… by Zach Lewis	96
I Hope the Herd Can Swim by Zach Lewis	97
Negative Callout by Keavy Rake	98
Peacetime Grunt by JR Miller	99
The Standoff by Kyle Phillips	100
Magnetized Compass Rose by Billy Whitworth	101
OEF to OAW (Redemption) by Andrew McFarland	102
TRADITIONAL PURGATORY by Katherine Dexter	103
Checklist by Chase McGrorty-Hunter	104
ballistic coefficient by Win Anderson	105
I am Win. By Win Anderson	106
Rome with WiFi by Joshua Landspurg	107
Proem based on 444 by Enrique Gautier	108
Mediocre Marine by Robin "Griff" Griffiths	109
90's Kids by DJ Sorensen	110
"Are You Still Watching?" by Allan C. Nunag	111
So Long by Phillip Mullen	112
"Were you waiting long?" by Jared Curran	113
If I Could Write Your Healing into Existence, I would by Alex Horton	114

A Dog as my Anti-depressant by Alex Horton 115
Thank you for your service by Alex Horton 117
The Hardest Part by Stan Lake 118
Red Bird by Dustin Jacobs 119
First Time Back by Evan Weaver 120
Michigan Procession by Chris Pimentel 121
Farah by Stephen Medrano 122
The Fall by Caleb Taylor 123
Victim-Initiated by Caleb Taylor 124
Fabric of War by Lani Hankins 125
Irony by Nate Didier 126
From someone who can't, forgive, forget by Michael Baumgarten 127
The Luxury of Forgetting by SquidXIII 129
Thousands of Miles Away (from HKIA) by Jonathan Pfenninger 132
I Cry Quietly by Gabriel Rodriguez 133
The Things We Learn by Shelby Edwards 134
Disposable Heroes by Brandon Casanova 135
Bonnie by Tyr Symank 136
Meditations on Knocking Off a Hat by N. Jed Todd 137
20 Years by Gabriel Rodriguez 138
Fond Regrets by Lucas Wood 139
The More Things Change by Mikael Cook 140
I didn't even know him by Mikael Cook 141
Feathers and Charges by Keavy Rake 142
Mesquites by Juan Flores 143
The Hammer by Mason Rodrigue 144
Dancing in the Abyss by Cyrus Norcross 145
A Child of Surrender by Neal Simpson 146
Sand in My Pocket by Matt Coffey 147
After War by Adam Magers 149
Rest by Amy Sexauer 150

"It makes no difference what men think of war, said the judge. War endures. As well ask men what they think of stone. War was always here. Before man was, war waited for him. The ultimate trade awaiting its ultimate practitioner. That is the way it was and will be. That way and not some other way."

-Blood Meridian, Cormac McCarthy

Poetry

I am no poet
But it seems to me'
That great poetry comes
From feeling or the poverty of it.
The poet, then, is the one
So scarred that feeling comes
Too much sometimes and
Too little at others,
Who keeps searching for words
That say what words can't.

There's this little orchid flower
In front of me,
Next to my laughing Buddha
That belonged to my Grandparents.
This little balled up flower,
Still shrouded in shadow.
It has one petal
Just beginning to open.
Like a chick, still asleep in its shell
Just waking for the first time.
It has many witnesses –
The Happy Buddha, the open blooms around it,
The sunset, and me.
Yet, I am the only one who cries
Because I am the only one who can.

I'm no poet. I've never read much poetry,
And never studied it.
What I am is a knuckle-dragging war vet,
Who aches and longs
To move from this dull, cold void
Into the world, so I might feel warmth.
I want to see this little flower open,
Its petals kissed by the Sun.
Maybe it senses my longing,
Or maybe we just share the same one.

By some magic
A second petal just broke forth --
Literally. The damned blessed thing just moved,
Sharply releasing its newborn tension.
Now, that's fucking poetry!
Without a word, this brainless newborn
Has outdone me.
Undone me.

I'm lost. My search for words is useless.
I'm like a heartbroken, drunken pirate
Wandering in the forest at night
Aware enough
To know I'm lucky to witness this miracle.
How can I describe this beauty?
This miracle? This longing?

I want to come home from war.
To be reborn.
I want to be seen, blooming and in bloom.

—Adam Magers

Mandala

As harrowing as combat
As lofty in its station
There's two things in this life I've done
One loving, one Forsaken

The first I lived when I was young
When wisdom was yet nascent
When myths of men and hallowed friends
Left scars both rich and latent

The second comes, and with it strife
My struggle to deliver
She tugs at every part of me
Draws love like blood; A river

If to Atone,
Those things I've done, I know not how I'd do it
But her eyes show that love is blind
This guilt, this shame; Undo it

To Life from Life
A solemn vow, the cycle yet unbroken
Her smile melts my lovelorn heart
In sunbeams 'pon the ocean

—Tamim Fares

Irony

At ten I saw the birth of this war from a fifth-grade classroom.
I watched the world as I knew it came crashing down in an instant.
Childhood innocence lost as I watched the bodies of the jumpers
Plummet to Earth before the towers fell.
At twenty I was fighting in a war that has been going on for
half my lifetime.
At thirty I saw the forever war end, with political promises broken
and dignity non-existent.
From a college lecture hall, I watched the people who could not hold onto the
C-17 as they fell to the Earth.

—Matthew Sabedra

80's in the Rain

i stood straight out staring
at the rains heavy fall
outside on the back porch.

it sounded like
a million flags
waving in the wind.

it smacked the leaves hard and heavy
with a slow concussion, one after another.
Sometimes stopping as they
were in order to readjust.

the 80s were sounding off looms
from a mud pit, behind a dirt wall and bags of sand
the iPod mini buzzing on the roof of the mrap
as moondust and marines sifted swiftly swept the compound

i jumped down with my rifle
tuning toward the front of our line
and spider Webb shimmered through
the trees as it will always do regardless.

they held strong, even through
it's punishment is determined
by where it sets up.

the rain became a heavier
bending the branches, water rushes through the gorge
out back on the porch, staring. Listening.

—Julian P. Seddon

wide asleep & sound awake

in dreams—
no.
nightmare's glare
follows me
into humid days.
sometimes—
well, no.
everyday.
I can't tell if I'm awake
smoking bones to the tape
where my words aren't real.
yes—
why? to be real? all states
is to be utterly confused
& controlled, until you
become aware you aren't.
so, I go back to sleep armed with my teeth you can see in deep hibernation, never to
talk with words again—unlearn it all.
allow privation to take over,
a sure set back, but not for fail.
it's the natural state.
for the human the most dangerous
animal is:
the brain.
sometimes, I have these moments where I'm in a strange place, and I have shoes on.
their always new-balances,
in both places.

—Julian P. Seddon

savages don't suffer

we spent all of our days
in the wide open,
behind small cover
with makeshift shade,
padded drums.
because before us,
there was no one there,
soon enough we'd move along
enduring, quietly learning the
imprisonment of pain
carrying the chase—
& the way it makes you
feel
steadfast & forever
hungry, standing along walls
under overpasses, in academia,
on the El, sitting in artificial air,
waiting, wanting to return
to the wilderness of grain.

—Julian P. Seddon

Two Bracelets

I wear two bracelets
one for a man
one for a dog
pieces of metal
reminders of a past
still present

daily sights
clinking sounds
engraved
with names and dates
flags and scrolls

light reflects
off worn surfaces
flickering flames
of lives gone
present
in their absence

guiding me
by the wrist
away from the wars
I've fought with myself

accessories of a selfish man
keeping my feet to the ground
I need these anchors
lest I forget
and float away

—John Garman

No Combat, No Problems.

You never fought.
I raised my right hand twice.

You never fought.
I deployed three times,
saw the worst
of humanity three times,
survived three times.

You never fought.
They broke my body,
She broke the rest;
I'm still a great parent - the best.

You didn't even fight.
I talk to gold star mothers
battered spouses
disabled veterans
and shellshocked friends.

You didn't even fight.
I listen to trauma and grief,
despondency and disbelief,
suicide and homicide.

I didn't have to kill
Or maim.
What a bullshit criteria
To proclaim.
I'm sorry you're so sad,
I'm not the one to blame.

You never came to visit.
We always took the time,
Even when we didn't have the time,
To visit.

I may not be the leanest,
Or the meanest,
Or the greatest,
Or the latest,
But I've seen a few things
And done a few things
And I know a few things.

Two enlistments,
Two children.

Always prepared,
Never conducted.
Honorable service,
Honorable Father.

—Jacob Szydzik

The Weight of War

I remember this day, in 2008,
As if it were yesterday.
I carried more weight
Than a twenty-three year old ought to carry.
Two-hundred rounds, a pistol, rifle, and armor
Weighed me down.
But all that was nothing,
Compared to the weight of an aid bag
And being "Doc"
For a platoon of my friends.

I feared more than anything
To be called on
To save one of them.

The memories
Of my friend's blood on my hands
Weightless
And yet it sank me
Almost into the ground.

Twenty-three year olds ought not
Carry such weight.
It's bad for the back, bad for the soul.
I can feel it still
As vividly as I do the gunfire,
And the bomb blasts
That tore through my body.

That twenty-three year old may be
Ten years older now
But that kid is still in here
Aching from what happened
And the terrible weight of war.

—Adam Magers

Our War

In treasure spent, countless.
Immeasurable liters of blood
turning all the poppy fields
into a quagmire of mud.

My brothers, my sisters,
sealed in black zippered bags,
to be sent home as cargo;
remembered with folded flags.

The masses have had enough...
forgotten why we're here...
and all of us old warriors
have spent a whole career...

doing the leaving, and shooting,
the breaking, and uprooting,
the bleeding, and grunting,
the relentless manhunting,

so you could sleep in bed.

So you would feel at ease.

Now all the pain and demons
haunting us
will not allow for peace.

We're right back where we started,
with more medals than before...
but less of self, we tried to help,
then died beside our war.

—Simon Paul Burke

Root Cause

I'm close, but not complete.
Not out, but know I'm going.
I can't wait to plant my feet
And finally start growing.

—Simon Paul Burke

sometimes i go away pt. 3

one time i went away, my love
off to a desert land
i went to fight and kill for you
but lost me in the sand

one time I went away, my love
lost in the crushing void
hand in hand with my despair
in hell we were both joined

one time i went away, my love
i left you in my past
began the long climb up and out
the void was closing fast

one time i went away, my love
but came back from the fray
it cost me everything i was
but i've finally learned to stay

—Steven Callahan

weather forecast on whether war's passed

rustburg, virginia
april third
two-thousand twenty-four at approximately 1206
it rained

hard and fast and
filled the divets
in my lawn
with muddy water

that seeped into my crocs when I
walked to the
shed it
pelted my windows and not

far from me
thunder rolled
like a great convoy of Humvees
in the clouds

the rain felt
like it would
never
end

now
several hours later
the sun is shining and there are only 3 stratiform clouds
visible from my office window

the rain has stopped
its over now
thank God
for sunshine

—Steven Callahan

this is my story, this is my song

If we ever meet again
somewhere down the road
where the story's plain
and the truth is told

where laughter lines crinkle
on our ancient face
and our old eyes twinkle
pruny hands embrace

with the dust set and
the war the complete
tears of regret
not tears of defeat

I'll pull you in and
squeeze you tight and
tell you its okay and
that I wish you love and light
and for you I do pray

if we ever meet again
somewhere down the line
where bitterness is turned to joy
and silence turned divine

I'll tell of a long lost hymn
sung by tongues of old
praising God our father
because now our tale is told.

—Steven Callahan

Perspective

I've scraped away the same soil as you

I could only imagine what it was like

A routine morning patrol taking point

Unsuspecting attitudes and vigilant awareness

You turn the knob and hear the screeching wail

Swing it side to side, over dirt and metal

You step out of the PB and go across the bridge

Blinding blue skies, lush green foliage, mud

You know where to go, so you pick the route

An hour or so goes by, everything as planned

Darkened soil, a freshly disguised intersection

Surrounded by stacked mud and narrow paths

Murder Holes scatter the walls from the years

Everything's an indicator if intended to be

Patterns begin to appear, aligning with the mud

Scanning back and forth to see who's watching

Your squad takes cover, watching all directions

You approach with hesitant confidence

Swinging back and forth, you get a strong hit

painting the image based on misplaced dirt

The sweeper screaming and pausing

All evidence leads to a metal cylinder

You take a knee and pull out your kabar

Yellow tape emerges, more with every scrape

walking the same paths

on that day

a stroll around the AO

knowing anything can happen

Detector in hand

ensuring it works

Looking up, a beautiful day

locals drinking chai

avoiding main paths

up until now

A choke point

no other choice

eyes everywhere

paranoia ensues

it must be

a trigger man

readying to kill

murmuring a prayer

eyes turn xray

seeing the device

warmer or colder

directional fragmentation charge

dug into dirt

And then it happens, deafening

A split-second feeling of dirt, plastic, and metal

A gut feeling of soaring and dropping

It rips right through erasing your consciousness

'boom'

vision simultaneous darkening

hitting your body

Flying, to never to land

all goes black

—Tom Headle

Marines die, it's what we do

Look, I made a promise
you see
to get everyone back
...and I did...
except for me

—Tom Headle

PURPOSE

It's not seeing death
It's not a lack of sleep
It's not a lack of pills
It's not losing friends
It's not…

It's living in the tension
It's holding grief while embracing joy
It's the almost
It's the both
It's the maybe
It's the what if
It's the and

Time doesn't heal wounds
Courage to process the wounds does

It's not the bombs
It's not the gore
That's what men are for
Give me a goal
Give me a task
Give me purpose
That's all I ask

—Jake Howell

Elegy for Khowst

As I round the turn at the West end of the runway
one last time, I look out over the sun setting behind
the Spin Gar, and behind them North Waziristan,

then survey the mountain chain as it runs
sadly East to the Parachinar, that salient where
Afghanistan meets Pakistan in an uneasy, public
handshake.

This was mine, once.

I feel the cool of evening settle down
on my shoulders, the light breeze wicking away
the sweat from my neck, blowing it off towards
the graveyard of martyrs from a far earlier war.

I continue down, past the hulks of airplanes left by the Russians.
I wonder what their vets would say? Would they laugh
at a folly repeated? I know we would, and maybe
we will when someone else comes here to fight.

Past the helicopter pad where we flew countless thousands
of times into valleys we could walk in our sleep after men
whose true names we'd never remember, not that that mattered.
They'd die just the same.

Remembering their names was for someone else to do.
We just knew them as objectives, made up names that allowed
an enemy to fit neatly into our charts, robbed of the humanizing
fingerprint that was their real name.

And finally past the memorial we built, to honor our own dead.
Almost 400, forever to be young in their pictures and in our minds,
lost for a cause ten years past being cared about,
but lost all the same.

Our dead who were their objectives, perhaps. But not to us.

To us, they were the martyrs of our own little war. Martyrs who mattered
only to those that fought here, and to the sons and cousins, brothers
and nephews who'd keep their story alive. Until the next time
someone comes here to fight.

—JS Alexander

A Coke and A Smile

The smell of water running over sun-baked
                        concrete reminded me of summer sun

sizzling on pool decks, reflecting over
                        girls, basking by the clear water, thinking

about what they'll wear that night, who they'll
                        call, or maybe how far they'll let a boy go.

Out of this reverie I realize the water
                        won't cut it, won't get the blood out no matter

how much we scrub. I know it's bad for morale to leave
                        the blood in the truck, and we have to go back out,

offload the casualties and jock back up, back into the fight.
                        So we scrub, frantically, Lady Macbeths

in tigerstripe cammies. Then CC remembers his childhood
                        dentist keeping teeth in a baby food jar filled

with Coca-Cola, how he warned him, saying see, see here?
                        Coke can eat through anything.

So we reach in the cooler and each grab a can,
                        spraying the gore away, cleaning the

side of the vehicle with acid rivulets of sugarwater

—JS Alexander

Meheranah (Manhood)

"Man was matter, that was Snowden's secret. Drop him out a window and he'll fall. Set fire to him and he'll burn. Bury him and he'll rot, like other kinds of garbage."
-Joseph Heller, Catch 22

Carrying the body off of the shot up
truck into the clinic

where the doctors would try to work
their miracles even though

they knew Gul Badshah was already
dead, his teeth hanging loosely

where the round had entered as he turned
to face his assassin,

we dribbled a trail of blood and clear
fluid that dripped from his head

through the sheet, onto the pavement, looking
for all the world like

the liquid dripped when you take out the trash
and someone has thrown away

a drink with something left in it.

—JS Alexander

RUCKSACK

He packed his ruck prior to leaving.
Painful memories and awful feelings.
Rolled, folded, tucked into compartments
He learned to carry the weight before.

He packed his ruck in uniform.
Loaded it with grenades, mines
and other things meant to take lives.
He carried a weight that was growing.

He packed his ruck for the mission.
Food, water, extra medical supplies.
HIs brothers had to lift him off the ground.
He carried a weight that was unwieldy.

He packed his ruck to go home.
Carried it with him wherever he'd go.
Unable to set it down on the ground.
Too afraid of the weight it carried.

He packed his ruck one last time
when he left the family home.
Carried it down empty streets at midnight.
Wishing he could relieve the burden.

His dragging feet caught a curb,
with force the ruck came crashing down.
Face bloodied. Buckles broken.
The rucks contents spilling out.

All the figures of regret and grief.
Seen now in a different light.
Unpacked. Unfolded.
Present in a different perspective.

—Chris Madsen

Forever War

They call it the Forever War,
War Forever.
War in every clime, and place, and weather
War comes flying on Bald Eagles feathers.
War for worse, War for better.
War ends- Never.
War in the West,
War in the East,
War in the mountains,
and jungles, and streets.
War in the most, War in the least.
War in famine,
War in feast,
War slaughters the lambs,
War feeds the beast.
War turns men
into bones
and meat.
War Incorporated suckling
at the War Machine teet.
War in the Future,
War in the Past,
War, Forevermore, is why peace can't last.
War for Country,
War for Kin,
Holy War and Jihad
for every religion,
War to make martyrs
out of men.
War can't be justified.
War is Sin.
War first fought
for survival of tribes,
War now fought
for politician's bribes.
War with sticks,
War with stones,
War with guns,
and tanks
with drones.
War with knights,
fought for Dukes.
War with the World,
ended with nukes.
War Forever
across all air,
sea, and land

War from California
all the way to Japan
War is the Natural State
of Man.
All War is Different.
All War is the Same.
War is the Constant.
War Unchanged.
War Forever makes life unstable.
War Forever since Cane
killed Abel.

—Mason Rodrigue

Easter

I sit at a dining table,
Surrounded by family,
We eat lamb and drink wine,
And laugh,

I look out the window,
A warm day with green grass and cloudy skies,

Beyond the garden lies a graveyard,
A grey trellis fence separates the living and the dead,
My mind pictures soldiers going on patrol,
Climbing ladders to scale the fence,
And depart friendly lines,

My smile has gone,
And my family wonder what is wrong,
I am back in the room,
"Zoned out" I say,

I can't tell them,
That the war is here,
And it's always here to stay,
It would be unfair,
To let memories spoil the day.

—Ben Fleming

Post Deployment Blues

I served
I fought
Yet was it even seen

I served
I fought
Yet was it even heard

I served
I fought
Yet was it even felt

I served
I fought
But was it even real

— Mary Garibay

fire resistant

it's 10:23 a.m. on a thursday
answer the phone with a smile
and try not to swear so much
but i am thinking about how
we were told to blouse our boots
in the motor pool and unblouse
when out on the road
back and forth, tuck and untuck
my pants were too baggy
and i didn't follow the rules
because garrison in a warzone
felt like a joke no one laughed at
ring ring, ring ring
auto-pilot kicks in and a voice
acts like any of this is important
but i am thinking about how
combat shirts melt into your skin
an accidental defect
a little whoopsie daisy
i don't want to smile
everytime i answer the phone
i want to unblouse my boots

—Ali Watts

Ode to CV

I never had much sense of smell except for polish,
perfectly round, black as a void,
a torn scrap of brown t-shirt
dipped into the dark cream and gently swirled
onto scuffed leather of worn-in boots,
creased and wrinkled in all the right places.

The trick was to mix it with a dab of water
for a spit-shine appearance without all the saliva,
and we did just that every night,
shoulder to shoulder,
after she worked the ironing and I folded the rest.

When we switched over to tan
they only required the occasional dusting,
but it didn't matter by then anyway,
because she was long gone, or I was long gone,
and we'd never sit side by side again.

—Ali Watts

Just Another Day in September

History and cultures
met with explosive force
high above the world
on a bright September morning

Steel and glass
lives and illusions
shattered in the blink of an eye

And in the aftermath
investigations
legislations
invasions

Must defend
must avenge

And another generation
of damaged youth
physically
mentally
emotionally

Thank you for your service

— Charles McCaffrey

OIF/OEF: A Haiku

So long and thanks for,
the sleepless nights and the kids
who hardly know me.

—Jason Green

Solid as a Rock

They lifted my abs out on the operating table,
they told me later that I must have been working hard
in the gym.

I could have died there in the Afghan sand,
where we left the gym equipment for the victors to
pretend to use.

In my mind's eye I see the wheel of the elliptical,
spinning as I lay on the mat late in the evening,
finishing a workout.

In photos I see the "liberated" clinging to the wheel,
of the last plane as it tries to leave behind a
plan that didn't work out.

—Jason Green

Down into the Dark

When you were swallowed
In the warm humidity,
and the roar of the stadium crowd,
A pale-faced, gawking, gibbering mob,
with their flags and buntings.
Artifacts, all -red, white, and blue.
You knew that they would not remember you.
Afraid and reluctant,
They cheered your journey
down, into the dark.
Then oceans away,
you-
detached and dreaming of ice cream
and cool carpet underfoot
hear those hucksters-
heroic in their mien.
jibber on about the myth,
and worshiping the avatars of your tribe
as they commit your future to
the dark.

—William A. Adler

The Air Was Red

The grey-green haze of ersatz rain
Filled our lungs as we strained
Our breathing echoing
The cracked metallic call to prayer.
"I will come to thee" fulfills a solemn hope.
So, it is echoed every day.
And on high, across the ancient mountains
and down along the soft-sided pathway
dun-colored ribbons of young men wandered,
to the caller's tent once again.
While a swirl of dust betrayed,
the devout observer
While the Lieutenant's people murmured,
like the sound of pebbles falling.
his headset crackled with the electric-static warning,
"The Air is Red".
Then, up again.
With the muffled muttering,
Such scene-
Our burdened men stumbling,
the fog of dust hovering,
and distorted shadows of men tumbling.
When that dark cloud sprouted from the dirt like a shroud-
It came with the sound
that "all the people may hear".
So the Lieutenant spoke his words aloud.
But the people stood far off,
and they trembled with fear.
So,
the Lieutenant approached "the thick darkness"
where God was.
And, there he knelt,
touching each one,
and in fear and wonder, he invoked
the Nine Lines-
a prayer.
But each one died.
Un-rescued on that mountain-side,
because the air was red.

—William A. Adler

My Nation's Warrior

I am my nation's warrior,
My life is in their hands,
Won't question when I'm asked,
To ply my trade in foreign lands,
Or hold the line at home,
When darkness pounds upon the gate,
All I ask for is remembrance,
If falling is my fate.

They were their nation's warriors,
But now they have returned,
They wear their scars inside and out,
And medals they have earned,
Some nights they wake up screaming,
Though their mind's too far to hear,
It's seeing, hearing, smelling, feeling,
Old, familiar fear.

I was my nation's warrior,
But now I march no more,
Now I'm left to question,
Do I know what it was for?
What all the blood and suffering,
Adds up to in the end,
What return on this investment,
Of our brothers, sons, and friends?

They are your nation's warriors,
Handle them with care,
They're dangerous, and vulnerable,
And they'll always be there,
So, protect them from the people,
Who'll wage war for greed and gain,
And remember them, their families,
Their sacrifice, their pain.

—Martyn Lees

Sandbags in the Hourglass

I enlist in the infantry at seventeen, I am sent to Fort Benning.
The hourglass tips over, the sand begins to slide.
"This sandbag has many purposes. It will save your life, it provides cover and concealment" my Drill Sergeant tells me.
I am sent to the Old Guard, ceremonial infantry in Arlington National Cemetery. A casket platoon.
My job is to carry the dead honorably, perfect, still.
On my casket team, we use sandbags to fill our mock coffins.
"A human body weighs about seven sandbags worth" my team leader Jon tells me.
"If I used to carry sandbags to mortar pits under enemy fire in Afghanistan, you can carry this casket to its grave."
Jon is killed in a motorcycle accident on the national beltway.
We carry him to Section 60 in Arlington. Jon loved to workout, we joked about how many sandbags he might be.
I carry the head of the casket, his weight tearing at my grip.
Eight sandbags, maybe nine.
We fly to Dover Airforce Base. It is Christmas Eve. We are to bring a recently fallen soldier home from Afghanistan.
"She was only 19, gunshot wound to the head. Heavy casket, be prepared."
Six sandbags maybe.
Years pass, I attend Special Forces Selection.
Tt is team week. My back feels broken; my feet are raw.
I carry sandbags through trails of hell in North Carolina until my grip bleeds. If I let go, maybe the pain will stop, but my team will fail. I never let go.
Two years pass, I don my Green Beret. I feel pride. Accomplishment.
I am in Afghanistan for six months, but I don't leave the wire.
I instruct my infantry on how to use sandbags for cover.
"This might save your life; they can be used to deter explosions on vehicles."
I am told to find sandbags to hold the memorial rifle stand for Andy and Ryan.
Our HALO team left in the night, they fought hard. They returned missing two.
I was supposed to be with them. I was taken off mission to provide administrative support.
It is winter in northern Afghanistan, the wind blowing strong on the flightline.
The spray painted black Ops-Core helmets and twin tube night vision glinting in the sun.
A formation of Blackhawk helicopters fly over after taps plays.
A helicopter breaks off.
We return home.
The hourglass is half empty, the sand still sliding.
Six months pass, we return to Afghanistan.
I load my gun turret hatch with extra sandbags, we will be out for eight days.
My hatch is an armadillo of death.
A 50-caliber machine gun, an M240 machine gun, a Milkor grenade launcher, my rifle, grenades.
We are ambushed, my right arm is struck with a sledgehammer.
My combat experience has begun, and it has finished.
The bullet impacts with no pain, although my arm continues vibrating.

I sprint with my medic to our support truck, the sky turns a dark red.
I feel the air split around my stomach as a PKM machine gunner takes aim.
My teammates help me on the medevac helicopter.
My sandbags are replaced by tiny clear bags of liquid surrounding me.
Ketamine. Dilaudid. Versed.
I spend a month in various hospitals, alone.
I can't feel pain, I feel empty.
I feel shame. I feel guilt.
The hourglass is nearly empty, the sands slowing in their crawl.
I spend the next five years battling arm complications, I face medical retirement.
My time is over, thirteen years and I feel left with nothing.
I begin to do the only thing I know.
I fill my sandbags.
I create walls of my own self-hatred.
I pour every memory of Andy, Ryan, Adam, Jon, Dom, Travis, Mischa inside.
If I can isolate myself, I can protect myself.
Maybe if I fill my sandbags, I will be alright.
I fill them with self-doubt, guilt, anxiety, shame, fear, sadness.
My girlfriend leaves me. I move to Colorado alone.
I can no longer see.
The hourglass is empty.
I have made a tomb for myself, marbled clean.
My time is over, there is no more purpose beyond this 31 year life.
America gave up on Afghanistan, why wouldn't it give up on me?
I watch my Afghan partner force be executed on Reddit.
They died for their country, and we died for them.
I failed, and there is no more purpose to my time.
I grab my pistol, I feel the cold barrel on my head.
I call my mom.
She talks to me, I don't fire.
In the next days, I pour everything I have into writing.
I look inside myself and I must accept what I see.
I see the younger me, proud of the man I have become.
I have only walled myself off from my own self-acceptance.
I tear down the walls I have constructed, I see light again.
If we build walls when we return to regular life, how could we ever see the light we have?
If we work ourselves to death, if we shut out those who love us, if we find every distraction we can, we never have to accept who we were.
In order to grow into the man I must become, I have to accept the man that I was.
I forgive the man who shot me.
I forgive myself.
Nobody is firing at me. There are no more caskets to carry.
I turn my hourglass over. The sand begins to slide.

—Alexander Tirabasso

Old Flame, New Fire

Our relationship – War and I – lasted seventeen years.
It started some time before we made it official.
I, watching from afar,
Transfixed, transformed.

Turned out to be toxic.

And now it's over.
Time to move on.
A new one is lying in wait,
I can feel it.

And yet…

And yet I miss the old, familiar smell.
The feelings and red flags I knew so well.
I want the nightmares I know,
not the devils I don't.

They will be so much worse.

—Dan Gimm

Depths of Bagram

Through the abyss of a sandstorm, I sunk
feet heavy with impact on the ground
stirring up ancient dust, Afghanistan.
Cold palace of concrete T-walls,
shrouded in the arms of a mountain range
foundations quaking in the wake of war.
Within, people are calculated, toy soldiers.

Father of ruins and jagged rock blasted by bombs.
Concealed secret of human design.
A smuggled jewel shattered.

This is an unholy dwelling, the locus:
a local farmer outside the perimeter holds the rein
of his camel watching as we wind up our backs.

—Jacqlyn Cope

Legacy

I wonder
if my girls will ask me
what I did in the war
when they cover it
in classes

and I wonder
how I'll answer them
if words will ring true
or be tainted
by this hindsight
that now haunts us

—Colin Halloran

The Global War on Terror is Over

It still pulls at my seams,
a stray thread caught in the breeze.
Echoes and shadows
chase each other along weathered walls.

"Can't wait to go home," I mummed once,
sitting on top of the rusted husk of a tank.
Memories crackles
like static through a broken radio.

Those scorched summer days,
We traced each other's footsteps.
Fear in our eyes,
thrill nestled between our ribs.

Now, some nights, love is the landmine.
Family a bustling street seconds before a blast.
Home a dull cage,
the bonds tighter than tangled razor wire.

It still pulls at my seams,
but I'm learning to sew a new tale,
a patchwork of stories and scars,
where each stitch bears its own weight.

—Don Mateer

In my Office

When the gates of HKIA crumbled,
grey dust settled over the medals on my wall.
A rug embroidered with the Lion of Panjshir still hangs,
its threads worn; its edges unraveling.
Beside it, the green, red, and black flag Abdul gave me.
A symbol of a country that exists in memory.
Abdul's been gone five years now.

On my desk, sits a photo of me and Darwesh,
thumbs up and grinning.
We were friends then.
Now the frame is cracked, the glass clouded with age.
I wonder if he still has his copy.
If he still remembers that moment.
If he's still out there, somewhere.

—Don Mateer

Memories of Sunset in Kandahar

I watched you depart.
Your lungs strained for air
but even the wind had turned its back on you.
Your final breath, a faint rattle beneath the darkening sky.
The sun leaned westward,
a weight of orange and pink sinking under its shroud.
Night stretched out its cloak. Tiny star punctured the taut canvas.
The breeze twisted dust into slow, spiraling echoes,
each grain a word drifting away. Time wove its cold tapestry,
thread by thread, toward the universe's darkening edge.
I brushed the bugs from your face, a last tenderness to the dead.
When my time comes, I can only hope
someone will swat away the flies
from my hollow eyes.

—Don Mateer

Pain into Purpose

Pain that is not transformed gets transmitted
My pain has been carried in the recollection of a memory
Bidden or unbidden, this pain I have carried for so long
For me, only through healing can my pain be transformed

My pain has been carried in the recollection of a memory
A memory of tremendous loss, grief, and rage
For me, only through healing can my pain be transformed
Pain echoed through time connected by our shared humanity

A memory of tremendous loss, grief, and rage
Through processing and healing, I can change the nature of my memory
Pain echoed through time connected by our shared humanity
Through meaning-making, I am transformed with purpose

Through processing and healing, I can change the nature of my memory
Bidden or unbidden, this pain I have carried for so long
Through meaning-making, I am transformed with purpose
Pain that is not transformed gets transmitted

—James Kadel

OverWatch

I was your overwatch on your first mission
Jacked up on confidence and ability,
Still fumble fucking over your own feet.
Your overwatch when you made daesh pray
To any God that would listen.
And even your overwatch
When you and the guys
Played light sabers
With your piss streams
Your overwatch when
The extraction bird went down
Your overwatch when
Whisper was useless
Your overwatch when you
Gave them hell.
I also had to watch when you fell.
Valkyrie, overwatcher of the battlefield.
Chooser of fallen warriors escorted to Valhalla
Overwatch of the overrun,
The overworked,
And under supported.
DOL

—Nicole Hughes

We Carry Our Brothers with Us

We carry our brothers with us, for our war is never over.
Only the fallen have seen the end of war, while the rest struggle to stay sober.
We carry our brothers with us, our scars never heal.
When we face the reality of war, this all becomes real.
We carry our brothers with us, we will always feel their pain.
So when I look my child in their eyes, I know the sacrifice was not in vain.

We carry our brothers with us, on our wrists and in our hearts.
Though I haven't seen you in a while brother, Marine's never grow apart.
We carry our brothers with us, on the tattoos on our arms.
When we received the tragic news, our compounds sounded alarms.
We carry our brothers with us, long after the fog of war is clear.
I miss you my brother, how I wish you were here.

For when you lay your cover down, on that cold basement floor.
I will pick that cover up, as you need it no more.
I will dust that cover off, inspect its tattered cloth and brim with a bend.
And I will put that cover on myself, rest easy now brother, report your post.
Your watch has come to an end.

—Jason Landau

Electric Love

Days of
blue, red, white, yellow,
purple, pink,
and gray.
Life continues to grab hold,
with so much energy.
Possible is possible
running my fingers over
the linings of her heart.
Sending electrical currents;
waking my
nervous
system.
A magical collaboration
of energy.
By plugging my fingers
into her heart sockets.
The realm of infinite love appears,
with flashes
of life.
To run wild and free
inside her heart,
turns to the heaviest of pressures
to be loved by her.
Stronger than times
of enemy
gunfire
and
rockets.
A sense of accountability
crosses, loops, twists, and pulls
on my arms.
As jolts of electricity
surge through my veins.
No longer an addict to war,
now addicted to her love.

—George Briones

Vision

These eyes
Who hath seen
Thousands of years behind
Thousands of years beyond
Focus now

To behold the colors
Gazing upon the beauty
Marveling at the grotesque
How they shine in approval
Bulge in disbelief

Upholding the lie, the truth
Signaling the attraction
Beaming the disgust
Projecting the fear
Exposing the deepest recesses

These eyes validate the heart
Who puts on exhibition the soul
Bad as they are good
Twinkling in the moment
They tell the whole story
Without words

These eyes look back
On the wasteland
Of our foolish war
Our impossible mission
To make everything right
For everyone and no one
How they haunt

These eyes look forward
Flushed with tears
For it is the same wasteland
Nothing learned
History unfolds
Every gory detail

These eyes close
There in the blackness
Is the arena of peace
Where thoughts settle
The universe hums wild
The heart beats lighter
So to slip away

A voice jolts open these eyes
Sleep when you're dead, ol boy
There is much more to see
A rub of these eyes
On they will behold
For however long

All is a gift

—Christian Sonnier

From Ship to Shore

It rocked me to sleep
Every night with a gun
Next to my bed. This metal
Vessell ached and groaned with
My clenched fists and heat-sweat
Skin. I built it and gave birth to it from
Every argument with my mother and every
Fight with my brother. I hated them. Wanted
Them gone. Yet it was me who disappeared
Instead. It was me who left home, never to
Be seen again. And now I'm on this ship
Pointing my anger at them toward the
Houses of my enemy. In holy war we
Trust that our country will
Bring us home on this ship.
When the tides and the lies
Stop, I am the gun, loaded for the
Spring to Summer erosion. The muddy
MarPat tide of heat-death. Everybody that
Falls is an erosion and their blood the new
Brooks and streams digging through the
Wild flowers near their home. Every
Night that I look at the stars, I pray
A silent wish for the wind to wash
Me away and all the anger and
Hatred I have left. But, that's
Not all that is left. I'm left
With the blue and water
Isn't blue. Not really. So,
What am I then?
When tide has
Broken against the
Shore, what am I?
The law of the shoal
Says that I have to leave

Something behind and I
Have to take something
With me. What do I
Take? The gun is
Gone, left on the banks
Of the base in the desert.
The water isn't blue, but I
Am. I'm the story too. I'm the
Moment in time and space that carries
Its sadness on its back and its joy in front,
Looking for the peace of me I can't ever get back.

At night, when I don't close my eyes and I'm not asleep
I still hear the ache and groan of the ship, and the wood
Sounds just like the metal, only less refined and
More personal, because I did it and I didn't.
I panic because I'm a witness to the
Slaughter and I'm too scared to say
A word about what comes next
For those who are next,
To go from ship to shore.

—Harry Foster

Midnight Movie Madness

At 12 years old, I cried when the credits rolled on
Saving Private Ryan, heartbroken by the loss of
Private Mellish. It was four minutes after midnight,
Past my bedtime, but my dad who had served in
The Gulf War lay snoring on the couch next to
Me. He'd fallen asleep before Private Mellish died.
He never heard my strangled cry of "no!" as
The German soldier slowly plunged the knife
In his chest. To me, it was a real good-bye.
One, I was ready for.

At 21 years old, I nursed a glass of vodka and tropical
Punch while watching the final minutes of *Jarhead*. It
Was just before midnight two weeks before deployment
And my roommate lay snoring in his rack, an audience
Of beer bottles watching him sleep. I wondered which
Marine I'd be at the end. Would I have a family? Facial
Hair? Work at a supermarket? A corporate office? As the
Slick and cool nothingness of the vodka dragged all feeling
Down into the depths of my subconscious, Swafford stared
Out the window of his beach house, wondering. It was a
Different kind of good-bye. One, I was ready for.

At 26 years old, I was the drunkest I'd ever been. It was
Eight minutes after midnight and my roommates were
All out partying. I sat with my eyes held prisoner by the
Horror on the TV screen. "13 killed in attack on Kabul".
It couldn't be. Why? We were there to leave? The fighting
And dying was over and we were just supposed to leave.
The screen said otherwise, a twisted reality show where the
Characters weren't real if you didn't watch the show.
It was the worst kind of good-bye.
One, no one was ready for.

—Harry Foster

Succeeding

Welcome Home Warrior, Welcome Home.
It's good to have you back,
From the far off lands you roam,
Afghanistan, Iraq.
Set your boots upon the tarmac.
Let our gratitude extend.
Lay down your heavy rucksack.
Although the journeys never end.
Recite your knowing poem,
A sonnet aphrodisiac.
Each story is a tome,
So pen your paperback.
May inspiration never lack,
To help us comprehend,
The battle and the medivac.
Although the journeys never end.
Swim and surf the ocean foam.
Break out the almanac.
Sleep beneath the starry dome,
That old familiar bivouac.
Sunrise follows nights of black.
There are mountains to ascend.
Stay off the beaten track.

—Michael Moriarty

Sonnet Of The Long Deployment

I penned you letters from the bitter front,
Where bullets flew and a few good men died.
The simple words writ by a lonely grunt.
When found alone again, you read and cried.

You thoughtfully wrote me, from back at home,
About holidays and good times I missed.
And then you sent that loving little poem,
About the moon lit night, that we first kissed.

When at last, the longed for day had arrived,
At our warm embrace I was excited.
You were extremely grateful I survived.
So fortunate, we were reunited.

For all of those involved, the war did burn,
Let's live well, for them, who did not return.

—Michael Moriarty

Find Your Meaning

Victory is in the moment.
Every day you face the grind.
Take the measure of your opponent,
Eternal struggle of the mind.
Rise to meet your full potential.
Aspire to achieve your dreams.
Need for purpose is essential,
Suffering is just the means.

—Michael Moriarty

All the Kings Men

We came of age watching the bodies that fell.
Zippo men, ten feet tall and bulletproof.
Twenty-four years, two generations of children to men.
Found what we were looking for-
A shattered, burning, bleeding, drinking, addicted hell.
Now it's time to go home.
It's time we go home.
We're not buying the flag anymore, no more pie to sell.

Those of us left have an ugly taste in our mouth.
The trench, the beach and the jungle doled their lessons.
Her majesty the desert gave us our own.
It's high time we left-
It's time we go home.
Your suit is empty company man, reap what you've sown.

We reached middle age watching the bodies that fell.
Humbled, standing tall and on the other side.
By our own compass.
We've found ours and it's real, now is the time-
Brothers and sisters, it's time we go home.

—Paul Hurtt

FPS

168 grains
10.89 grams
No love
No hate
Purpose and intent
Focus
Life and death
At
Two thousand, eight hundred
Feet per second

—Jake Hutchinson

Conex Boxes & WiFi Hotspots

Not a stubble in sight,
On the young boy's visage,
Just a grin & a twinkle
As they march off the plane.
The adventure is here,
That his country promotes,
Risking his life for theirs,
Or so it's been told.

Thanksgiving night,
What a wonderful time,
Until the mortars start falling,
Angry and loud.
The illusion is broken,
The adventure undone,
This is not fun and games,
That was somebody's son.

Scared of the sky,
Mostly at night,
Nerves are on edge,
The twinkle is gone.

—Lucas Wood

The Many Few

Bold men tread lightly on rocks
jagged and rough and black as coal
stirring the ashes that never smolder
burn and rage and grow like fire

Deep are the thoughts that run through them
the winds that carry yet never cool
burn and rage and grow like fire

So many before faced their fears
many after will follow close behind
for, war is not kind to eyes that see
a picture fading
a shedding tree
they are the frames born from embers
burning with rage
and growing like fire

Do not leave
as if to say goodbye
return as one
prepared to die

burn…
        rage…
                grow…

as if fire is beneath you

—Ryan A. Kovacs

Things Left Unsaid

We said goodbye
not see you later
yet, it still feels like
we never quite said hello.

we mixed words
like sodium in water
until we boiled the bonds
which held us together
leaving behind
the salt in the wound.

I can't tell which part of you died
because, for so long
it felt like we were living.
                                               in the moment.
                                for each second.
                  on top of the world.
with no stopping.

no one told us when to go.
we just, went.

        You

                just went.

like your words
that fell on deaf ears
it occurred to me
you knew what had been coming
because you were always so good
at going.

—Ryan A. Kovacs

Estranged Heading

Life was simple, black-n-white,
To live was to kill, to love was to kill – first,
That life, oh, that one I belonged to,
Is over.
Now that lensatic compass spins,
As I look,
To navigate this life of colorful contradictions.

—Matt Hayes

Looking Back

They said; it's better to be judged by 12,
Than carried by six.
And I wondered who would be,
The other three to carry me.
They sang; you should burn out than fade away.
And all I have to say is;
I wish somedays,
I went out with that bang.

—Matt Hayes

Home

The crack of gunfire echoes in my ear.
The potency of black powder flares within my nostrils.
I see the gleam of the Hindu Kush mountains;
Purple in color,
Red in strife,
I feel at home again.
Then I awake in a sorrowful sweat,
the short burst of dopamine fades.
The Living are gone;
Yet,
The Dead sit beside me

—Jake Pique

Dried Ash

Blow it all out with the smoke.
Dead brothers,
Crying mothers.
Joyful cries,
Sullen rhymes.
Electrified bars,
Unseen scars.
A child's innocent sight,
A warrior's endless fight.
Burn it out in the ashtray.

—Jake Pique

Beginning, Ending

It began with death
Carried by the winds of war
Ending, behold the rot

—Michael Baumgarten

GWOT Fever

The cold marble desk,
Elbows sit upon,
Teacher tells us so,
Planes have reached the awn.

Tears some hath shed,
Others look upon,
TV on its wheels,
Images far from gone.

Some will take the oath,
Others look away,
Who will take the blame,
A question not in frame.

—Christopher Brown

Trending

Oh, excuse me,
I didn't realize my war
Wasn't trending anymore.
Seventeen years
Must be too
Long to store
Another violent conflict
For you to abhor.
Yeah, it's raw
And still feels sore.

Oh, don't apologize,
I'm in disguise.
Don't you don a mask
To hide your
Weeping eyes?
Charred children
Amputated.
Ambulances
Filled with kids.
Daddy fell off a plane
As he gripped the skids,
His body smashed
Into asphalt
Exploding snot fluids.

Twenty years of war
Are fresh on your mind
But not like mine.

—Benjamin Fortier

You Were Just…

You raised
Your hand
To defend a land
That would take
You for granted -
Just like I did.

I looked down
The bridge of
My nose
Not seeing
A combat badge
Like those
Of us
That have.

I forgot we
Didn't pick
Or choose
We just tried
Not to lose
Our friends
Our will
Our sanity -
My pride
Got the better of me.

I was broken
When I judged you.
I said,
"You were just…"
And that was wrong.
Because you belong
Here with me
Side by side.
We are family.
For some of us,
It's the only one

—Benjamin Fortier

Who Did I Kill?

Who did I kill with glee in my heart?
A farmer? A father? A son taking part
in defense of his village? To whom was imparted
those small copper rounds with evil black arts?

I hope they were vile; devils from hell,
rapists and thieves deserving expelling
or rotting hot death while their corpses would swell
(but if you were wond'ring - yes, they died well).

We trampled their bodies, we slogged through their blood,
and not even once did we wonder it odd
that we laughed as we shot at the image of God
who, compared to our sins were perhaps not so flawed.

I've heard it was said, "Lions don't cry
over prey in their jaws." Perhaps that is why
questions abound for lambs such as I
who made these brave men stumble and die.

—Cokie

The Duel

My king and lord, we've been at lines
for days and days on end.
Our swords feel rust for lack of use,
and patience starts to bend.
The fields and flowers, grass and roots,
grow weary of our tents.
With soil and rain, they call for blood
and long for nourishment!
The men sing songs of going home
before they've drawn their steel,
some showing truth of fearful hearts
that waiting has revealed.
Upon my oath, these men of ours,
they seek the peace of slaves
while drums of Gauls on distant plain
turn brave to timid knaves!

But hark, my Lord, to battlefield!
Some mischief is at play!
From foe-men's line rides forth a man
who longs to fight today!
At last! The scoundrels sent their man,
their champion of war,
who calls for us to send our own
to try upon his sword!

Let *me* cross swords with such as he,
I beg my Lord and king!
My shield hand burns! My blood, it yearns!
My blade, it longs to ring!

Oh bliss that I might clash and strive!
In gratitude I ride
that I might hazard Fortune's hand
to risk my head and pride!
And as for thee, my enemy,
defiance shall be met!
For each alike to kings, we owe
this debt of blood and sweat!
I'll take thy head, I'll burn thy standard
here for all to see
I'll drive this blade into thy heart
as thou would'st do to me!
A laugh, my fearless Frankish foe?
as thou dismounts thy horse?
I hate thy blood, yet love thy joy
through worthy veins so coursed!

That one should die so all might live
like Christ upon His cross,
that roaring lions die for mice,
that gold might burn for dross!
To men like us, a noble death
shall be its own reward,
so come, my sudden, newest friend -
we dance the dance of swords!

And should we die, both thee and I,
and each one slay the other,
oh find me in our heaven's gates,
embrace me as a brother!

—Cokie

Christus Rex

"The gates of heaven are lightly locked,"
yet gates of hell are tightly barred -
for fear of kingly, holy Christ
and potency of His sacrifice,
the minions quiver at their guard.

Advancing lines of Christendom
pull battering rams. They set
against the doors of Satan's host,
who mew their sickly, fearful boasts
while quivering in sour sweat.

The common gods of common man,
roost upon their ruined thrones,
and at each golden trumpet blast,
as power of the Lord roars past,
they moan a coward's moan.

The psalms and songs and praises are
the missiles of His providence;
For blessings on the lips of men
could cloak the beggar like the thegn
in prayers of frankincense.

Those whose martyred hearts recalled
what martyred flesh cannot -
His joyous seal upon their souls
would buoy up those in darkest throes
and fan a blaze from dimmest coals -
this even Satan has forgot.

So they that wait upon the Lord
now soar on eagles' wings
while grounded evil strives to fend
off waves of God that bind and rend
their sickly fortress built on sand,
surrounded in a ring.

Though evil forces once would feed
on fear of fallen minds,
now dragons eating dreary ashes,
starving while the battle clashes,
trampling their shrines.

Can desert stones avoid the sun,
or fish avoid the sea?
The inevitable dance of God's advance

holds evil's gaze like prey entranced
while Christ is King of all-expansive
conquering royalty.

—Cokie

Green Monster

It is more than a wretched notebook.
Its contents filled with thoughts, deadlines, doodles, quotes, AAR's, and lists.

The bindings wish for reinforcements.
Covers swollen with water-colored green stains from spilled coffee
Pages fanned with writing, leaving the notebook half-open

That green monster has seen the world as I have felt it.
It has consumed my experiences of every rank
It has been a blank canvas for all things 'important',
It has been tabbed out and ferociously abused by my surroundings, handwriting, and thoughts.

It is a part of me, and what I have done.
When the pages run out, I will add it to the collection of other used and abused green monsters.

—Brooke Bottensek

Salty

The pinch sinks as I do.
I fail to fill my hourglass.
I turn upside down. Water runs—
past perspirations—crystals
remain. I think my sand-
paper is too coarse.

                        The salt
from my skin I flick like a scab:
So what that I've been there?
So what that I've done that?
What remains but the stained
outline of all that I spent.

—*Camp Shorab, Afghanistan, 2019*

—Olivia A Garard

Five-Star Google Reviews of the Green Beans Cafe at Kandahar Airfield

1.

Best damn coffee in the AOR.
Great spot, a little civilisation in the void.
I mean pretty good for its location.

2.

Hot!!! Coffee.
This place was literally an oasis in the sandbox.
A super ok location for militants!

3.

The coffee?? So-so.
Free Wi-Fi and Bollywood is a bonus.
Service is good, if the power is on.

4.

Need Caffeine? In a war zone? This is the place for you.
A MAGIC place.
Never been.

5.

Better than Starbucks.
When given 1 option, it's the best option.
I had to enlist to get coffee from here.

—Olivia A Garard

autec

flying again over—bahamian blue
waters and the c-one-thirty descends
fast, to a bumpy, stop. potholes
on the airstrip. customs slow,
the detachment jammed up—
in the shack, ladies frying conch
fritters, men dominating dominos.
glass of switcha. jitney pulls
up, palm trees and strange roads
welcome the navy's area
fifty-one.
weapons training for pilots, hunting
submarines in the tongue of
the ocean. loaded seahawks with hell
fire missiles, lightweight torpedoes,
and a billion sonobuoys.
smash goombay smashes—
everyday at the light house, or
beach house, or thousand fathoms,
not an alcoholic on andros island.
first time, sip sip, white hennesey
and drunk driving golf carts.
don't tell chief or we won't
make it off base to barbeque by
the blue hole with a rope swing.
avionics checked, left hangar bay
paced to the bar. master-at-arms
pissed at who conquered the shuffle
board table the past two weeks—
hot tequila later, gaze on cosmos,
indescribable and unidentifiable
green light zipping around, other
worldly.
hungover ride to the jetty,
carrying masks, snorkels, and spear
fishing poles. splash
transparent water, rainbow
coral, eels, turtles, lobsters,
crabs, rays, and a trillion fish.
climb ladder of algae, barefoot on jetty,
ordnance team chatter, nato exercise
with port visits in the u.k,, inevitable
deployment to the mediterranean,
and the next goombay smash.

—Caleb Durden

The Vines

The last time we spoke, we did it beneath the vines.
Two tired men, just winding down time.
We spoke of home, and the plans that we had.
Of our deployment, both the good and the bad.
With pale light piercing through our tobacco smoke, we found time to dream and a moment to joke.
Now I know you'll never come back home, to this place in the pines.
But you'll always live on laughing, at our spot beneath the vines.

—Rodolfo Garcia

The Other Side

I used to live inside those gates, but no more.
Still, I stay close to keep the sounds of
gunfire and artillery from fading,
and the choppers overhead.
I may not have the life I had, but being here makes it feel
like it is all within reach; like I could have it all back,
if that was what I truly wanted.

Some days I am glad I left and start to feel like
I am getting settled into this life that feels new, but isn't.
However, it seems the moment I start to accept
being a civilian again is when
I hear the cadences rolling down the trails
and see the rucks floating through the mist.
When I begin to believe I am ready
to leave that old life behind
all I see is the uniform that used to be my life
sitting at every table, standing in every aisle,
being what I used to be.

Even went as far as marrying a military man
and while that did bring me closer to the wrought iron
and eventually beyond the tangled metal mass
that locked the world out,
in true Army fashion that man was sent away,
leaving me alone.

I had believed if I could have it back within reach
I could let go of all the bitterness and anger
that I was still carrying around like my gear.
But during one night out, just driving around,
I found myself sitting outside the
barracks where a fellow soldier had killed my dream.
That was all I needed to drop the pain on the curb
and finally come to terms with the fact that
there is no going back.

All the times I assumed I wanted the life
that would restore the worth I thought got left behind
was, in the end, just more wasted time.
So much had changed since I was last there
making me a stranger to the place I love and hate.
I still live where I can hear the gunfire and artillery,
and keep the choppers overhead.
The difference now is that I am at peace,
or as much as I can be,
with the life I once had beyond those gates.

—Lani Hankins

(Untitled)

How did it end?
(did it ever end?)
I still dream of the rugged mountains
I still long for the tense quiet
The infinite stars.
Questioning suspicious eyes that warmed over time
(many of them kept us safe)
The women.
The children.
Oh the women and children.
It was presumptuous to dream for you.

—Demere Kasper Hess

On Reading...

I read Tim O'Brien in high school as a result of defiance for my final essay in AP English
I ventured into more Tim O'Brien after boot camp
Followed by Junger, Marlantes, and Remarque
Empty because I have never experienced their wars; never even experienced my own generation's
However, I gained an appreciation for never having to experience the hardships and loss of the people who's lives I've lived through their words
But I still find myself reading O'Brien as if I'd never seen the silver lining

—Zach Lewis

I Hope the Herd Can Swim

Now that my generation's conflict is over
The grasp for relevancy begins
Old traditions take over and the pursuit of the next enemy becomes an anxious fixation
Once I realized the cycle continued
It was too late to swim out of the whirlpool
And at the bottom of those turbulent waters, that even I contributed to by brutishly following the herd around me
Nothing matters, too much, because I hear there's big changes coming

—Zach Lewis

Negative Callout

Fighting, forbidden.
Fumbled exit, foreshadowed.
Warriors, restless and anxious.
Forced Peace, watch them die.
Can't leave, we're not going back.
Be rich, in this place of the poor.
Orphans of partner forces, gazes averted.
FOBs, destroyed.
Defilement, denied?
Dust and remnants of teams past.
Cacophony of chaos, echos of silence.
All that remains.

—Keavy Rake

Peacetime Grunt:

I missed the war I thought
Eyes caught
On the same two bricks Next to the metal door Barely donned a uniform And I missed the war Shaken by the realization That I had no inclination Of how I'm to be a soldier Now that I missed the war All I'd heard were stories
From the ones who'd gone before And I'd done nothing
Yet still
I missed the war Born too early
Or perhaps too late Unnerved by the fate
Of having lost my proving ground Since I missed the war Embarrassed by my service
And all the things I didn't learn Wearing a cord
I'd never get to earn Because I missed the war Maybe that's better
That's certainly what some will say But I have never felt
The crunch of red dirt Beneath the sole of my boot Never known the dry heat

Or learned the hard truths Of a hateful world
Since I missed the war But I do know the shame The feeling of a boy Playing dress up
Amongst a world of better men With no chance to defend
The tribe of calloused hands All because
I missed the war

—JR Miller

The Standoff

Your eyes are like a still pool of water
Reflecting back the fear that outshines the blue
That winter beard is getting a hint of grey
Only zits sprout from mine like so many of your home's mountains
Your gnarled hands braced on your hips, lips pursed, a curse loaded
Mine braced on the turret to stop the shaking
You were born in this village
I was born in a room larger than your house
Your boyhood was spent fighting the Russians
I played soldier with sticks that looked vaguely like guns
You speak a language that's trapped between the mountain passes
Mine spreads over the world like a fog
You'll walk these roads until your sons bury you
I'll patrol these routes until my tour is done
After we are both long gone, we will have had one thing in common
You wanted to go home
I wanted to go home.

—Kyle Phillips

Magnetized Compass Rose

"It is"
I said to the ghosts
Of what became known as the ill equipped
In a coliseum of conversations

Then a tunnel
Unremarkably dark
Yet unfamiliarly kind
Not claustrophobic
Because chaos doesn't fear anything
Just for the time being, small nest so fragile

I remember dancers
I remember song
I forgot the words
Because none of it was real, all along

Don't mistake my silence for disregard
I just don't know where I am
And the synapses are forbidding me to stand
I disguise

This is treasure
Self-preservation
Damn, what a nice lighter
I'm a survivor

I think I was once somebody
I knew I would always be nobody
It was enough being in a body
Sometimes my soul doesn't even want that
The will to live is being mischievous and naughty

Then to digress and repress

I'll take my chances here
In the present collection of moments
That amplify and augment fear

I'll bear a tear
Smile for the sake of being alive
I've lost my need to want to die
To continue, I'll try

—Billy Whitworth

OEF to OAW (Redemption)

A call comes in from the TOC and we head to the trucks.
We get on our kit, load up, and our convoy rolls out.
No need to go fast, the streets are crowded with hordes of kids anyways.
They stare in awe of the big trucks and the Americans in their uniforms. Some wave and smile while others cower or throw rocks.
The men's stares are different though. Military-aged males in tiger stripe BDU's and soccer jerseys look at us with hate-filled eyes.
Maybe they've seen us before. They could've been the ones selling us cigarettes in the bizarre or trading us pens for bread a decade ago.
Maybe we've never met. After twenty years of conflict, they likely heard some horrific stories from their elders. The experiences of their fathers or grandfathers passed down from one generation to the next.
We were sworn enemies before we even knew of each other's existence.
These elders are harder to read. Their indifferent stares are distant, cold, and blank. They stand unwavering in their man-jams and pakols. Some missing limbs or appendages, displaying old wounds from an old war.
They don't have the same burning hatred in their eyes as some of the younger men do. When these men stare, it feels like they're staring right through you and there is no looking away.
You can see another look in their eyes as well, something we all feel too. The tension and the uncertainty. We're all trying to see how this is going to shake out, and how much we can really trust each other.
For the most part, it looks and smells and feels just like it did over ten years ago. The difference now is not only the mission, but the location.
After the fall of Bagram, over 10,000 ~~refugees~~ allies landed on our doorstop, on American soil, and our little piece of the world changed overnight. This was a new phase of the war, one that we never saw coming.
We went from providing suppressing fire to fire suppression. We were no longer running gun trucks in the Middle East, but fire engines and ambulances in the Midwest.
Every day brought back the feelings of being in country. Reliving the hard times, longing for the camaraderie, and mourning the ones we'd lost so long ago.
It took years to bury all those feelings and memories, and only a moment to bring them all screaming back to the forefront of our minds.
The good thing now though, is that it's over. All of it.
Thousands of Afghans were cared for and relocated to new homes across the country. Soldiers returned to their garrison, and civilians went back to work and their daily routines.
Over a decade after we thought our part was over, after almost two decades of war, it finally felt like it all had been put to rest.
It felt like our mission was truly complete. It almost felt like redemption.

—Andrew McFarland

TRANSITIONAL PURGATORY

My therapist
is all the extra sleep
I could talk to someone else
but who knows me
better than my dreams
So I smoke a little weed
I take the socks off of my feet
I crawl back in
these stale sheets
and pray that all my needs
recede
How do I speak
Where do I go
Who understands
who really knows
What I once was
was someone else
disappearing in the smoke

—Katherine Dexter

Checklist

1. Shave off all my hair
2. Learn to shoot a gun
3. Become a man
4. Leave everything I've ever loved
5. Get my chance to die
6. Try to kill someone
7. Come back to a broken home
8. Have hate for everyone
9. Try to reintegrate
10. Fight to put down the gun

—Chase McGrorty-Hunter

ballistic coefficient

we are just
human beings being human

when we shake hands.
with crinkled eyes locked;

pupil is a wormhole back
through eons continuum.

spacetime warps wraps
around iris in oval

blossom. with one hand on
bosom, the other extends

stretching out as timeless
projectile segment filaments

pulse as if in osmosis. plasma
fluid flows back contracting in

    a singularity
dark as a pupil

that no one escapes.
still we shake.

—Win Anderson

I am Win.

I did twenty years in the Army.
Five as Infantry, fifteen as an Aviator.
I deployed to Afghanistan five times.
Writing helps keep the demons at bay. Barely.
I have published one book and two poems. Previously.
I am married with two kids, two cats, one dog and one wife.
Usually you can find me hunting or fishing.
Bring beer.

—Win Anderson

Rome with WIFI

Does history repeat itself? Can we learn from Rome's mistakes? The future is now. We can make a change — it's not too late.

Protect the border, invasion by the masses. We welcome immigration but are swallowed in waves of refugee classes.

Billionaires pull their strings, the middle class shrinks, very few feel the financial sting. These political puppets sell their souls, their righteous voice is shouted while they amass wealth not backed in gold.

A country divided, no, not the north and the south. The vulture's wings are red and blue, peasants keep fighting while the circling predator sees the plan through.

Overreach, overextend. A military might can only control so much, the numbers dwindle, it grows tired, it thins.

Before the fall, the greatest empire on Earth was rotting from the inside. Are we too prideful to know that could be us, the land of liberty, Rome 2.0 with WIFI?

—Joshuah Landspurg

Proem based on 444

i swear
(without faith—)
to consent combat

without—
will,

without faith—
to defend *the* constitution.

without— affect,

without faith—

without—

which

I SWEAR
So brave are dead

—Enrique Gautier

Mediocre Marine

Boy becomes Marine,
just regular infantry!
What more could he be?

—Robin "Griff" Griffiths

90's Kids

We were
Just kids
Rocking M4s & M9s
Bringing fire from the skies
Foreign places
Foreign faces
We obliterated
Running from
A society
Uncaring
Unkind
Mothers and fathers
Weeping for
Lost sons and daughters
Now we've come back
To a home
We scarcely recognize

—DJ Sorensen

"Are You Still Watching?"

Recalling accounts.
Accosted constantly.
Conditioning our consciousness.
Accumulating the belief
that we Cost less.
That worthiness is debatable.
Reoccurring reasoning.
Retracing our mental steps.
Like a movie
you wouldn't
recommend.
A constant reminder
Asking…
        "Are you still watching?"

—Allan C. Nunag

So Long

so long.
so long from now till we are together again, if ever.
so long have i wished for days like this to never come.
so long, the distance between you and i
so long will be the days without you by my side.
so, long as you endure, i can endure, too
so long as you can stand to love me, i will love you.

—Phillip Mullen

"Were you waiting long?"

Let's talk about
the hole
that you died in.

I do not recall
the scent of it.
Only what you looked like.

Reaching
for the sunshine.
I knew
that it was too cold
for you.

Your muscle and skin
blending in
among the flowers.

Frantic and gasping.
And blinking.

Alone in that place.
Unaccountable to the final things.

Slow passing,
and your heart opens.

And I wonder,
was anyone there for you?

The last frame.
Calmed by repose
and shuttered.

This is it, and so.
I stand.
You lay your goodbye.

—Jared Curran

If I could write your healing into existence, I would.

I had a buddy who once said
if you leave this day with just one thing
be grateful for your toes.

His voice bellowed so loud it unhinged my beating heart.
Looking up from his military grade metal legs
his smile of gratitude a white flag of sacrifice
I could not yet grasp onto.

Staring out over a crowd of soldiers
missing parts of themselves
only God herself could see.

Those who's brain didn't tick the same
let their head hang heavy.

And their loved ones who stayed home
to receive their motionless flag of surrender
let out a sigh so deep
it made the grass blow cold.

Leftover in the crowd were empty shells
in uniforms that could still smell the ammunition
of failure ringing in their ears
and their buddy screaming over the radio,

"Bosco, run"
And so, we ran.

For most of us we ran so fast we didn't look back
until the wrinkles on our hands began to deepen.

Because looking back meant
seeing the blood underneath our fingernails
and the hands that we still had, and you didn't.
The laughter that we get to enjoy, and you don't.

Looking back meant

on most days

Just being grateful for our toes.

—Alex Horton

A dog as my Anti-depressant

The day your paws hit the Pacific Ocean
was the day I remembered
what it felt like to come home.

Your smile bouncing off the tips of each treacherous wave
like a four-year-old girl
who just circled around the cul-de-sac for the first time
on her rainbow bright bicycle.

Mother cheering her on like she had just witnessed a miracle.

You were my miracle.
And in that moment, I remember wishing
that chasing the ball into the waves made me feel as calm as you.

Joy doesn't come that easy to the rest of us.
We've been too busy calculating the outline of what
the mirror image might look like.
Picking between filters, half placed identities,
and violent souvenirs handed to us by our fathers.

Images we packed away in the bottom of our rucksack.
The same rucksack we carried off the back of the C-130
to the place where the smell of livestock
mixed with human decay shook our spine loose.

The place we ran away to

                or towards
   or at
                    with white knuckles

                             clenched around the only form of communication

                                      we grew up knowing

Rage, we expunged on faceless men.
Under pitch-black desert nights.
Nights filled with shooting stars
that could write a symphony with their light.

And then you became the only light I had left.
Your bark was my security alarm
that took all my nightmares away.

Your entrusting lean was what kept me

putting one foot in front of the other

        Until finally

                I could stand alone.

—Alex Horton

Thank you for your service

Thank you for your support   the words fall off the tip of my tongue   as the years tick by   and still I seem to be picking up parts of me   quivering with vicious teeth and screams   in the shadows permanently   I look back at old photographs   and all I see is a lifeless stranger staring back at me

A distant memory.

protective armor   piled layer upon layer   trapped in your greed   you paid for me   jaw clenched   eyes hollow   my ego screams   You cannot break me   You taught me how to be   You see   what is you   is me

I have killed you. just as I have killed me.

You made me your monster   so when you thank me   to clear your good conscience   my dear friend   how silly   because we are all on the wrong side of history   label me to clear me of my sins   moral injury & ptsd   new names but still the same horrible hostility

Humanity's disease.

Why is it that we refuse to see   we are collectively culpable   no matter where the siege   connected we all are   and will always be

You see. I am you. and you are me.

—Alex Horton

The Hardest Part

The hardest part
Of a forever war
Is when it's all over
And you look around
And see your brothers
Broken more from life
And the burdens they carry
Than any hardship
From that deployment
Seeing them spiral
From disappointment and death
From the stress of combat
And the cruelty of life
They were once the light
That couldn't be extinguished
And now just a flicker
Reduced to a diagnosis
I pray those demons
That have hijacked their brains
Go back to hell
And return the soldiers
Who would charge through fire
Just to feel the burn
The hardest part came not from war
But when we returned.

—Stan Lake

Red Bird

Listen, I'm not good at this.

I want to tell you Mom passed.
A few weeks ago.

I brought you this pin of hers.
She wore it every day after you left.

Not a Gold Star.

But a red bird, a Cardinal,
your favorite when you were a kid.

She wanted me to leave it on your headstone.
She missed you.

I miss you.

I also have a red bird pin. I'll never take it off.
See, here it is. The red is fading a bit.

I'm just going to sit here with you for a while,
I don't like leaving you alone.

The Washington Monument looks nice today,
the grass is real green too. I think you'd like it.

I'm sorry I'm not very good at this,
I'm just going to sit here quietly.

And I want you to know I'm ok.

I want you to know I'm ok.

—Dustin Jacobs

First Time Back

Fog wisping so slowly,
but too fast, and not fast enough.
Maybe it was just relative to the overload of...
four or five days of travel.
First time seeing green Maine pines in 10 months, or more.
Shocked me to tears in my plane's window seat.

So small, but looked so safe,
wrapped up and snuggled tight.
Maybe was just relative to the overload of...
no safety and only the snugness of my armor.
First time seeing a baby in 10 months, or more.
Shocked me to tears in that charter bus seat.

Older, they seemed, by years and not months,
thinner too, both. When they stood to meet me.
Maybe it was just relative to the overload of...
being unsure their son was actually back.
First time seeing my Mom, my Dad in 10 months, or more.
Shocked me to tears in that rental's back seat.

The same it seemed, and probably never will change.
Fought and fraught, again and again.
Maybe it was just relative to the overload of...
being back there, again.
Not the first time feeling the plane pitch hard.
Shocked me awake, but not to tears, no window in that seat.

—Evan Weaver

Michigan Procession

It's the same.   It's from the manual.
They pull off.   We pass.
They line the sides.   Some have waited hours.   Some passing through.
Same faces. Same Serious. Same Scare. Same simmering stare.
Always they look frozen, wooden, cutouts;   we're inching, crawling, winding.

I'm mostly in the front, the maps, the plans, crackles from the air.

The middle has relics,
        Some food, some weapons, some special tools

You're in back when it's your turn.
        Facing only the past, protecting, searching.

—Chris Pimentel

Farah

As I was lifted away I knew I would never return.
So I closed my eyes and said goodbye to the piece of myself I would be leaving behind.
My physical footprints would eventually fade as my spiritual gait would evolve to hover as a guest above the surface.
My undisturbing movements will become ghostly as I explore the waves of a civilization's time.
In the final moments, I opened my eyes to see the fading image of myself standing below,
and I called out to me, a thought that made its way from deep within.
Remember that the sunrise and sunset of Farah belongs to Farah
and we will be allowed to see it come and go through the borrowed eyes of its people.

—Stephen Medrano

The Fall

I watched from afar as, first,
The outpost was consolidated:
Demolished, blown to pieces,
A footprint of what used to be,
An island of security amidst a sea
Of violence and uncertainty,
Swallowed by an ocean of apathy
And strategic short-sightedness,
Lost forever like a diseased limb
Severed from a healthy body,
At least the body remains,
Infested, but intact,
A pruning, more than amputation,
But the tissue proved to be necrotic,
The sickness spread,
More outposts fell,
Decaying skin masked by Our might,
Like infusions of healthy blood
To a dying man,
We sacrificed to the end.

—Caleb Taylor

Victim-Initiated

What sorrow and sensitivity,
Softness and sadness,
When dreams that once meant elation,
Now drive me to despair,
When the thought
Of stepping out of the wire,
Deep breath inhaled,
The freshness of the air,
The warmth of the fighting season,
The hunt begun anew,
The nearness of death,
And so close to that,
The electricity of being alive,
At the pointy end of the stick,
Where all acuity is attuned,
To shapes under the earth,
Textures of the dirt,
Newness of the soil,
Concealment of the pressure plate.

Now, in peace,
These same dreams drive
Me headlong to agony,
To irritation and irrationality,
To fear, the stink of it
Surrounds me as I sweat
Through my bedsheets,
And launch myself from slumber,
With dread apprehension
Of the walks to come,
The time beyond the walls,
Where life is measured in steps,
And steps weigh more
Than the weight set upon them,
When the air sizzles with death
The death I once chased,
Now chases me,
Stalking at every turn,
Hidden in the treeline,
Behind the murder hole in the wall,
At home, loving and beloved,
I await my final footfall.

—Caleb Taylor

Fabric of War

I can't tell you what it is like
to watch men die in a firefight,
but I can tell you how it feels
to take the brunt of the anger
that lingers after it.

I don't know how it feels
to be under attack,
but I can speak about the anxiety
of being left behind
to wait for men you love
to return.

I have nothing to say about
war outside the wire,
but I know enough about the
torture and cruelties
that occur within.

I carry an improper story of battle
because it lacks the
explosions and spent shells,
carrying only remnants of
betrayal and psychological warfare.
I may have no scars worthy of
heroic tales or remembrance,
but I house wounds that
bleed through the ages.

I will never be
what others have been,
but I am woven still
into the fabric of a
perpetual war.

—Lani Hankins

Irony

They sent us to wash the blood from the truck
so we wouldn't have to keep seeing it…
….to erase the horror of the day.
But now I will see it every hour of every day
for the rest of my life.

—Nate Didier

From someone who can't, forgive, forget

We said never forget.
Not knowing what we were demanding,
To be shackled forever to the past.

Some pull the weight of flag draped boxes,
sworn to never leave someone behind.
Some build lonely villages,
filled by memories of long-lost friends,
kept haunting bar room halls,
glasses raised before leaving again.
Some went down in battle,
some just wasted away,
some of them even became heroes,
in common cause,
the same struggle,
how to start life over again.

Willingly they did answer,
estranged from those who did not.
Placed on pedestals by some,
their ears assailed,
shouting over broken pieces,
bickering over what it all meant

We are a nation moving faster,
trying to outrun, what we cannot escape.
Past losses unacknowledged,
and a defeat too easily dismissed.

So, we find comfort in victories,
carved in margins,
in places we couldn't pronounce.
All washed away in an instant,
just as violent as when it began.

What lingering tragedy did we bestow?
At the reading of our war's will,
the same gift we were given,
a machine that only knows how to kill.

Stones will be quarried,
hewn from mountains of aging war tales,
masterfully they'll be sculpted,
so as not to disturb our sacred beliefs.
Hollowed out, they weaken,
to collapse on whoever comes next.

If freedom means forgetting,
let it be granted to all who have lost,
go forth and chase better memories,
see without war shaded eyes.
I know peace may seem ever illusive,
when your pillow gives no respite.
Let yourself slip beyond fear's hesitation,
released from needless regret,
use what their life has bought you,
make the world grateful to know that you lived.

Let the monuments and graves do their duty,
It is here I relieve you at last,
with your torch, I will keep a vigil,
tell me their story, kept close to your chest.
Give me the coins and I will pay their way,
to cross the river at last,
forever welcomed and cared for,
an eternal well-guarded rest.

Now go seek life with all the vigor,
where you were once willing to die.

From someone who cannot forgive or forget,
so, you must do so instead.

—Michael Baumgarten

The Luxury of Forgetting

Forgiveness is a luxury for those who can forget.

I remember every day.
Every mother-fucking day.
Every fucking morning.

I remember
And remember
And remembered.

Sometimes trauma flashes
Like in the movies

Sometimes trauma is all-pervasive

All-day memory
Unshakeable
Unsquashable

The beef grows
The meat rots

I know the fear of rape.

The same fear
That creeps
Into
Every
Woman's mind
When walking alone
anywhere.

The threat of ego death
Or destabilization
Is very real

Anger grows pitchforks
Will justice ever find an ally in truth?

Did any veterans
take rifles to their throats
because
I was taken off the playing field?

Because I wasn't there?

Because my brains too fragile to

Shop for groceries
Enjoy beauty
Have a healthy sexual life
Eat a meal
Without

40 mg Prozac
100 mg Viagra
300 mg Wellbutrin
420 mg Green Crack

Keep me from
Headbutting
A wall

Viagra in the mail.
I know who is to blame.

It wasn't the one brought
the reality of rape
to my soul.

Leadership
So thoughtful
After
The trauma of an almost rape
And
Provide me with a day off.

You must be a stupid
motherfucker to get fired
on your day off.

Everything changed
I wish I could stop remembering

Forgiveness is for those who can afford to forget.

Active cases.

Abandoned without notice.

No pinch hitter.
No follow up.

The choices made
Trust betrayed.

The heartless phone call

On the day off
After a sexual assault.

We no longer need you
to prevent veterans from
killing themselves.

Broke my brain.
Scratched the record.
Solidified the previous day's
Horror

The music no longer contains hope
Or beauty
Just memories
Which invade
Conquer

Shackled on the other side of the subconscious.
I don't want to hear my screams anymore

Everyone smiled
Feigned comradeship.
Tainted accountability

Balls to the wall,
Drawn and quartered
Visceral irony.

"They weren't supposed to hire you."

Cute complacency,
Oblivious accountability,
Biased apathy

A great philosopher once said,
"I hate that I can't say "I hate you" to your face."

—SquidXIII

Thousands of Miles Away (from HKIA)

We watched them leave
while behind a screen
To serve thousands of miles away

We worked day and night
to track and support
Evacuations thousands of miles away

We (I) made calls and
coordinated for enabling Soldiers
To fly thousands of miles away

I (We) watched
as the pressure increased
Exploding thousands of miles away

My heart felt that day
how the actions I take
Effect lives thousands of miles away

It's the closest I've come to
sending someone to die
Thousands of miles away

—Jonathan Pfenninger

I Cry Quietly

I cry quietly before the sun rises
I cry quietly when it's the darkest
for the ones I will never again see, I cry quietly
I cry quietly so they are not forgotten,
for their families
I cry quietly because they are gone,
because I am here
I cry quietly until the sun rises,
until I hear the patter of little feet running down the stairs
I cry quietly until then

—Gabriel Rodriguez

The Things We Learn

We learn to make our beds, corners perfect and too tight for sleeping so
we learn to sleep on the floor, learn to sleep anywhere.
We learn, again, the alphabet—alpha bravo charlie delta echo foxtrot
all the way to zulu—
    an entire Army talking Romeo & Juliet forever, dancing tango.
We learn to use the radio, relearn speech, learn to love the clear static,
learn to say break, break and control our breathing and enunciate,
learn to love the invisible life line that is one radio talking to another.
We learn to read a map, if we didn't already know,
learn to match map to landscape, learn to measure our steps to the mile so we can
walk *quiet* off into the unknown and come out the other side
exactly where we wanted to.
We learn the act of war and rules of engagement and codes of conduct.
We learn how to dress, how to polish, how to roll our socks and how to stand,
properly.
We learn to crawl and run and the difference between cover and concealment.
Learn camouflage and movement to contact and bounding overwatch.
We learn the difference between passive voice and active voice and shed the first.
We learn to pay attention to the small things, the smallest things, to notice.
Learn to hold very, very still for a very long time.
I held still long enough once in hole just my size under a sky full of stars,
a field mouse came and sat on the toe of my boot and took time to smooth her
    whiskers and watch me watching her through the green of my night vision.
We learn to, and do, grow strong.
We learn to serve, a nation, each other, we learn purpose.
We learn to be your lethal instruments.
And in the end, we learn to forget, enough.
And we walk, quiet, out the other side and come home again.
Draw straight lines in the garden. And dance.

—Shelby Edwards

Disposable Heroes

Faces fill the spaces between awake and sleep
Laughing, crying, some just trying to torment me
Some frozen in fear by the death that they see
Pain in their eyes, remembering the lies, a line of tears falling to the side
Men with silver spoons sending them to die
Men with stripes and bars and shiny emblems on their shoulders
Motivating unorganized boys to move boulders
Showing videos and singing songs, encouraging these young boys to clap along
Getting in step they start to feel strong
Little do they know they're chanting their own death song
People line the streets to cheer them along
These lonely boys start to feel like they belong
Back in buildings with ivory columns, people with red or blue ties under their collars
Squabble about where they are going to send the American dollar
Little concerns about whether they are sending these men to heaven or hell
Just about whether their coffers are filled well
They may hear about the deaths and wounds,
 and that some come home with horrible stories to tell
They have nothing to fear though
For them it's a easy to make more disposable heroes

—Brandon Casanova

Boonie

The ramp drops and we rush from the school bus with rotors
Bodies and weapons slamming into the wall carved from the mountain.
We know you're going to light us up with that belt-fed
"Mullah Rahkmudeen, he's known to carry an RPK"
Afghan and American alike, eyes danger wide, excited smiles then laughter
Adrenaline drives us up the mountain, against gravity and death
Not a single shot fired
We flip baskets, shelves, finding nothing but frustration
Did you know? Or was it the echo of our advance coming up the mountain valley?
A beat up cricket hat sits by your gear. The Taliban Boonie.
If I can't find you, I'll take your combat soaked hat.
Maybe they'll tell you, "the bearded doctor, we see him wearing your hat"
Maybe you'll be angry. Maybe you'll step out with that machine gun.
Maybe I'll kill you.
Years go by and I'm here again, with your hat.
The mission numbers change, and so have we.
Numb, less forgiving, less clarity, more resolve.
Less interest in patching holes you made, more in making them.
They give me tasks, what's important to them.
I'm here to reunite you with your hat.
I've made mash ups to remember your name.
Mullah ROCK-ROCK, he's tallilicious.
They never let me get to your valley.
Another decade. Another life. Another war.
Once more to the graveyard of empires.
Your hat sits forgotten in the archive of black plastic footlockers
Between missions, I study imagery, read the reports,
tools we couldn't have dreamed of 15 years ago
"Maybe this route..." "If we had come from the north" "An LP/OP..."
I'm sent somewhere new for an emerging war.
Unrequited love for your demise
Home. Years feel like a century.
Black beard gone gray.
Hate turns to hurt, life to love
I'm rebelling against my warrior ways, fighting the urge to chase
He comes from the basement
An old tan floppy hat on his head. The grommets are rusted,
Silver glint tape safety pinned to the top catches the sun.
"Dad, is it cool if I wear this?"

—Tyr Symank

Meditations on Knocking Off a Hat

My daughter used to knock off my hat
When I was going into work
Or if I came home too late
Hadn't taken off the uniform
It was like she blamed the clothes
Or didn't like what I'd become
When I wore my Army duds
Sometimes I didn't either
Came time one day at last
To take it off one last time
One final ceremony, one last salute
She finally knocked it off for good

—N. Jed Todd

20 years

Yellow footprints
Getting on line
Running
Pushing
Left face
Right face
Forward
To the rear
Sight alignment
Sight picture
Squeeze not pull
Breathe then squeeze
Eagle globe and anchor
Green uniform
Cover on high and tight
Salute

—Gabriel Rodriguez

Fond Regrets

Jet fuel and filth,
The smells I can't forget.
The nights full of terror,
A rocket's silhouette.
Hallowed moments of laughter
That brought tears to my eyes.
Looking back fondly
On times uncivilized.
The best times of my life,
But also, the worst.
I can't be the only,
And I can't be the first,
To look back on these memories,
As a gift and a curse.

—Lucas Wood

The More Things Change

My 7th grade field trip consisted of climbing walls and falling towers. I reached for the last hold on the rock-climbing wall when the teachers shriek made me lose my grip. I tumbled down the wall before the rope and harness gave an abrupt halt. On the TV, we watched the bodies fall, no rope and harness to save them, each one hitting pavement.

20 years later, our desperate Afghan partners reached for the last hold on the wheel well of a C-17 as it ascended to nearly the same altitude the first tower was struck. We watched the bodies fall, no rope and harness to save them, each one hitting pavement.

—Mikael Cook

I didn't even know him

The final time you die is the last time someone speaks your name.
I stood at attention among strangers as his citation was read.
Veterans from every walk of life gathered for community,
We heard heroic stories of his life as a lump grew in my throat.
He wasn't here anymore but he brought us all together.
A lot of vets had a him, but he was ours,
He helped us heal,
We didn't need to know him.

—Mikael Cook

Feathers and Chargers

I vomited violently.
Spilling my liver.
Soiling the tent.
Fevered delusions.
Wakefulness evaded me.
I held the Pashtun baby down.
Covered in days-old shit and infections.
He screamed; I comforted him.
Needles pierced his flesh in unison.
He sobbed. I rocked him.
He fell into slumber, limply.
Then I was covered in shit and infection
He was no longer terrified.
He's going to America.
Alone.

—Keavy Rake

Mesquites

Walking next to crooked trees, a sense
of calm & reassurance breaks through
the oppressive heat of deep South Texas.
The Mesquite, leaning and bent
thick brown and red bark inches deep,
its roots 20 feet deep into the cracked ground.
Surviving,
still standing tall, against gravity
proud of their scars, thoughtfully
cut and pruned to its current shape
surviving hurricanes, floods, and
the oppressive heat of this arid valley.
Yet - no dried out turtle shells in sight.
Just peace,
laying on this hammock between two mesquites
I admire their strength and resilience, their
tall and curved branches breaking the sun's rays,
the wind, giving much needed relief.
I thank them resting under their shade
for relief and a calm mind.

—Juan Flores

The Hammer

They asked "Who will swing this Hammer?"
and we answered the call.
We went to War,
and they went to the mall.
The Hammer was Heavy.
The Hammer was Ours.
For 20 years we swung the Hammer
for the stars and bars-
We were the Spear that killed.
We were the Shield that guards.
We swung the Hammer,
no task was too hard.
For two decades we lost the best of us,
All that's left is the rest of us.
We didn't question whether or not it was just-
we mattered to each other, so it mattered to us.
Governments recruit kids
to fight their wars,
when children die
they shrug their shoulders
because they know
they can get more,
they don't even
have to tell us
what we die for anymore.
You may say it was for nothing,
you may say it was in vain-
but I won't let you shame their honor,
I will make you say their names.
If we do nothing about it
then we are the ones shamed.
It's time to call for accountability of the machine
from which our hammer swingin' gained,
the criminals who used our deaths
for political gain,
the snakes who gave lip service to our service
for their own fortune and fame.
It's time to unite and say to the ones
who created this hell-
Here's your fucking Hammer,
next time swing it yourselves.

—Mason Rodrigue

Dancing in the Abyss

Where are the ones who said they would be there, call me should you need help
No response, not word one word of encouragement
You're just a drunk Indian, a bum fuck veteran
Inspiring words from a brotherhood, just another warmonger to the public eye,

Roaming the street with bottle in hand, come sit with me a homeless man says
Tragic back alleys tales are exchanged, the audience all roaches,
Tossed into jail once more, there is no one to trust anymore
One look in the mirror, guilt and shame cover me like a warm blanket
What have I become, This is not who you will become

Alone in this world, this big bad world
I cried for help, but no one answered
Pistol in hand, one bullet in the chamber
Raise to my head, finger on the trigger,

This isn't how you go out you know, you're come back arc is about to begin
My reflection speaks, it is time to let it all go
I fall to the ground, I cry for help
Rock bottom has come, a stumble in the road
You're going to be okay, You're going to find life

Traveling to numerous places, speaking with strangers knowing life's mysterious
I grow to understand, I am the help I seek
I control what I allow myself to do, I embrace a simple way of living
Letting go of what has been, open to what is to come
Invitations to parties arrive at my feet, opportunities to break my will
Words of belittlement and jealousy tossed at me, from those who were once me
You think you're better than us because you're sober, I remember all your mistakes
I can not control what they think, I control me so I stay on my path

Solitude is ever peaceful, silence liberating
The blanket once warm, is now hot and burdensome
I take it off and throw it away, I am the help I need
People ask me for support, life changing questions
Words of encouragement come from the drunken Indian and bum fuck veteran,
Pain has been all I know, it has provided me the best lessons in lifeAlone in this world, this big bad world

—Cyrus Norcross

A Child of Surrender

War carries with it a thousand miseries
held aloft on soot-darkened wings,
an Angel gliding amidst broken dreams.
Each burdened beat
drives away hope held in closed hands,
spoken through clenched teeth.
Youth's last breath,
the final rise of a brother's chest,
we are all Children of Surrender.

—Neal Simpson

Sand in My Pocket

There's more steel in my toes,
More blue in my jeans, and
More pounds on my waist
That I'll just try to hide

No more HESCO's or heat strokes,
No more "are they good or bad?" folks
Don't feel like I'm in danger
Even though I tried

Well that free air is brushing
The lines in my face,
And my wife asks me
What I'm thinking about

I say the songs here are sweeter
And my clothes, they look neater
But there's sand in my pocket
That just won't come out

And the fields dance and wave in the wind
Where there's no war, famine, or drought
Well my tattoos have faded
And I'm a little more jaded
'Cause there's sand in my pocket
That just won't come out

I guess all the missed birthdays
Made a month of Mondays,
And that's math that just don't
Bear thinking about

You can keep all your goodbyes,
All the disappointed kids' eyes,
And that damn bus ride
Fighting with your own self doubt

And the fields dance and wave in the wind
Where there's no war, famine, or drought
Well I turned in my gear
But kept some of the fear
'Cause there's sand in my pocket
That just won't come out

At the time, I couldn't wait to get home
Shouldn't miss being back there, I know
Sitting there pondering your fate

While you hurry up and wait
But time turns your glasses to rose

From Helmand to Kuwait,
You love it and you hate
The hell, or the drug,
Or the simpler time

You miss the friends you rag on,
Or you're chasing the dragon
That beats the hours that you
Spend training online

And those fields might be just in my mind
If there's no war, famine, or drought
Well my language is cleaner,
But I'm still a bit meaner
'Cause there's sand in my pocket
That just won't come out

When your scars they stop showing,
Well life keeps on going
'Cause that sand in your pocket,
It just won't come out.

—Matt Coffey

After War

After war, we weep
If we are strong.
We lie down on the Earth
Trying to listen for it's heart beat
While our own hearts drum in fury,
Tigers growl, and our flesh
Wrenches from torture.

After war, if we are strong
We give up the fight
And we surrender to nature.
We let vines weave their fibers
Through our bones and muscles
And birds make nests in our
Empty, aching hearts.

If we can muster this courage
We will hear those tiny, frail chicks sing.
New life will find itself
At home in us again,
After war.

—Adam Magers

Rest

Strawberries grow over a tombstone
And I think I would like that

I use to prefer the idea of ashes
Which liberated my loved ones
From loyalty to a plot of land
Here the sounds of the city are not far
Howling through the trees
Echoes of the world that keeps turning
There is no uniformity
Unlike the massive fields of fallen soldiers
I have seen many times before
Would I rather lie
Free from individuality
Shoulder to shoulder with my
Militant brethren
Or beneath a quite
Unassuming stone
And shaded by a tree that outlived me
While strawberries
Sweetly creep along my resting place

—Amy Sexauer

"If people bring so much courage to this world the world has to kill them to break them, so of course it kills them. The world breaks every one and afterward many are strong at the broken places. But those that will not break it kills. It kills the very good and the very gentle and the very brave impartially. If you are none of these you can be sure it will kill you too but there will be no special hurry."

-A Farewell to Arms, Ernest Hemingway

About the Authors

William A. Adler chose a career of soldiering after college. He served for over thirty years as an enlisted soldier and as an infantry officer in places such as Bosnia, Kosovo, Iraq, and Afghanistan. When time allows, he captures some of his experiences, and those of others, in short prose or poetry.

JS Alexander is a former Special Operations Marine and current Diplomat with service in Iraq, Afghanistan and Ukraine. He has a BA from the University of Virginia, and an MFA in Poetry from Bennington College. His work has appeared in Consequences, The Wrath Bearing Tree, Salvation South, The End of the World, and War, Literature and the Arts.

Win Anderson retired from the Army recently. He writes a lot, though in fits and starts. He's published a few things, although none of it's any good. Mostly he likes to be outdoors getting up to no good in the wilderness. Somehow he has managed to stay married through five deployments. He must just be that charming.

Michael Baumgarten served in the Army for 11 years as an Army Ranger. He finished his bachelor's degree in Anthropology at California State University Northridge in 2021. Michael is currently working on his PhD in Evolutionary Anthropology at Arizona State University.

Brooke Bottensek is an active duty Captain in the United States Marine Corps, stationed in San Diego, CA. A Texan native that enjoys expressing military experiences and interactions through writing.

George Briones, Recon Marine, channels his warrior ethos into writing and creativity. With a blend of grit, resilience, love, and a profound insight into the human spirit, he navigates the transition from full-time warfighter to a passionate advocate for life through his words, using his pen name MX Geronimo.

Christopher Brown is a Retired Army Major and OIF/OEF Veteran. Chris has previous work published with O-Dark-Thirty, the journal for the Veterans Writing Project.

Simon Burke is a Former Intel, fortunate enough to retire from JSOC. There were many great times, but toward the end all he could see was the damage. He wanted to spend the rest of my life positively rebalancing the karma. Now he's an Infrastructure Development Project Manager, and with the free time he can eke out, he writes, hopefully that becomes full-time someday.

Steven Callahan is the third most interesting man in the world. He once mud wrestled mud itself and was victorious. He dressed up like a Marine for one weekend a month, two weeks in the summer and seven months in Afghanistan.

Cokie is a vituperative redneck who marinated in a seminary, then performed the obvious transition to military service. After doing bang bang things for pew pew people, he picked up a pen and discovered it was significantly more convenient than the sword. Despite (or because of) multiple blows to the head, Cokie continues to use the Oxford comma.

Jacqlyn Cope, an Air Force Veteran, Chicana, and MFA graduate who teaches at LAUSD. Published in Wrath-Bearing Tree and Collateral Journal, she serves as creative non-fiction editor for the latter, and currently seeking publication for her memoir. Her memoir, *Flower of the Dead*, explores breaking generational curses amid connecting and bridging her cultural, feminine, and veteran identity.

Jared Curran is a poet from the four corners region, specifically the southwestern portion of Colorado. After a decade long tenure serving as an infantryman and EOD technician in the United States Marine Corps, where he was engaged in multiple combat deployments, something happened. His mind, his heart, they shifted. They changed. The diverse and complex people that inhabit this earth inspired him to become something greater.

Dex is a mother, a writer, and pretty ok at most things as long as she's seen one tutorial. She has a finite amount of good behavior and most of it is saved for her children, so they can learn to be decent human beings, or at least not violent criminals. (so far they're just doing petty tax crimes)

Nate Didier was an US Army Infantry NCO with C. Co. 1-133rd INF, 2/34th BCT deployed to Nuristan Province, Afghanistan from 2010-2011. He has previously been published in Culture Cult Press' Spring Offensive: Poetry of Strife and Spring (2023) and the Right Hand Pointing's The Law of Forgetting: Poems on Moral Injury (2023).

Caleb Durden is a technology consultant for the State of Mississippi. During his Navy enlistment, he served as an aviation electronics technician stationed at HSM-48 in Mayport, Florida. He holds a bachelor's from Ole Miss and is pursuing an MPA at Tulane. His debut fiction novel is The Mizoquii.

Tamim Fares - Seven years, two deployments, and lots of questions. Chief among them: what now? Nearly fifteen years after coming home for the last time, an answer - of sorts. Her daughter now exists in the world and therefore; so must she. Ruck up and keep moving. Life is to be celebrated.

Ben Fleming served 16 years in the British Army as an Infantry Soldier in the Princess Of Wales's Regiment (PWRR), serving on operations in Helmand Province, Afghanistan. He is committed to changing the narrative around post war Veterans, through stoic philosophy, mental fitness and alternative therapies but above all else, a relentless pursuit of life beyond war.

Award-winning poet **Benjamin Fortier** enjoys playoff hockey, gardening, and playing guitar. His poetry book *Phantoms* has been recognized for its poignant portrayal of combat in urban Iraq.

Harry Foster served five years on active duty in the Marines as a Combat Engineer. He graduated with a B.A. in English and Creative Writing from Columbia University in Spring 2023. Harry is now a graduate student in the English department at Michigan State University, studying comic books and superheroes.

Olivia A. Garard served as an active-duty Marine Officer from 2014-2020. She is a member of the Military Writers Guild and tweets sometimes at @teaandtactics.

Rodolfo Garcia was born and raised in central Texas and joined the Marine Corps shortly after high school in 2005. He deployed in support of OEF 3 times (2008, 2010-2011 and 2013). He is currently stationed in Hawaii and is set to retire at the end of 2025 after 20 years of active service.

Mary Garibay was born and raised in the Inland Empire in SoCal. Happily married with 3 children. Served in the Reserves for 11 years, while serving was part of the Navy Funeral Honor Detail team out of Riverside National Cemetery. Then deployed at the peak of Covid19 in 2020.

John Garman served in the 75th from 08-11, during which deployed a few times as an FO with CCo. He is now training as a psychiatry resident in Pennsylvania.

Enrique Gautier is a poet in Denver, Colorado. A veteran of the GWOT conflict. He is persuing an MFA in creative writing from Naropa University where he explore's language fluidity and instability.

Dan Gimm has been an Engineer Officer in the Army Reserve for over 18 years and on AGR active duty for the past ten. His war was spent leading construction operations throughout Iraq, Kuwait, and Afghanistan. He is currently an ROTC instructor in New England preparing future Army officers for the next war.

Jason Green is a retired Army veteran of the wars in Iraq and Afghanistan. He holds a B.A. in Multimedia Journalism from UTEP and an M.A. in Professional Creative Writing from the University of Denver. His non-fiction has been published in As You Were: The Military Review, vol. 16; Proud to Be: Writing By American Warriors, vol. 11.

Robin "Griff" Griffiths joined the Marine Corps infantry after 9/11. Served with first battalion second Marines for two deployments to Iraq, first with Task Force Tarawa during the invasion and then with the 24th MEU in 2004. Griff was severely wounded with a week left on his second deployment but now lives happily in Utah with his wife and kids.

Colin D. Halloran served as an infantryman with the US Army in Afghanistan. He has since published three collections of poetry about war and PTSD, Shortly Thereafter, Icarian Flux, and American Etiquette. He is pursuing a PhD with a focus on war poetry. More information can be found at www.colindhalloran.com.

Lani Hankins served in the U.S. Army as an automated logistical specialist. She is a veteran of Afghanistan and former female engagement team member. Lani currently resides in the Flint Hills of Kansas with her daughter where she works as a visual artist.

Matt Hayes was in the military from 2008-12 with deployments to Iraq and Afghanistan where he was blown up. Few accolades are worthy, but he cherishes the 1st place wheelchair-basketball certificate for 3-85th W.T.U. Ft. Drum N.Y.

Tom Headle, a Marine Corps veteran with two tours in Afghanistan, now resides in Denver where he works as a Readjustment Counselor, helping veterans navigate post-war life and heal from trauma. His poetry, drawn from personal history, aims to offer insight and solace.

Demere Kasper Hess is a US Army Reservist with combat deployments to Iraq, while active component, and Afghanistan as a reservist. She recently turned to poetry as a form of cathartic processing, helping her balance her roles as mother, wife, and Soldier. She resides in Maryland with her husband, son, and blind cat.

Alex Horton, an Army SOF combat Veteran, led the Cultural Support Team program during her ten-year tenure in Special Operations. She played a key role in the selection of women within Special Operations. As an I/O Psychologist, Alex now works as a leadership and psychedelic integration coach, supporting Veteran healing. She was also accepted into Sarah Lawrence's MFA program.

Jake Howell enlisted in the Corps in 2006 and deployed to Iraq in 2008. Since then, he has gotten married, become a father to two girls, earned a bachelor's, a master's, and a law degree. He is honored to have his poem "Why I Run" published in *War... & After* and a short story, Claustrophobia, published in Vol. IX of Lethal Minds Journal.

Nicole Hughes was an Army E-4 15W turned military contractor for USSOCOM as their ISR officer. Four spins across the pond. Iraq (Al Taqaddum, Al Asad) and Afghanland (Helmand, Mazari-Sharif , and Nangahar) Left in May of '17 after finishing up overwatch for the MOAB in Apr.

Paul V Hurtt is a small business owner and GWOT Army Vet. He was there at the start and watched it all burn. He was a dirtbag his entire time in. He drank and partied his way between deployments with zero thought for the future. He lifts and he writes.

Jake Hutchinson is a dirtbag saki guide, avalanche forecaster and mountain rescuer. He trains search dogs, wander deserts and explore rivers and canyons of the Southwest, trying to fill the insatiable curiosity of what lies around the next bend.

Dustin PK Jacobs is a United States Air Force veteran who retired in 2021 after 22 years of service. He served as a missile maintainer supporting B-52 aircraft GWOT operations, and as a mechanic working on nuclear intercontinental ballistic missiles, and national security space launches. He currently resides in Montana.

James Kadel is a combat veteran who served 20 years in the US Army as an Engineer officer with two tours to Iraq and two tours to Afghanistan. James currently resides in Washington state and hopes to connect with other combat veterans through art, music, and poetry.

Ryan A. Kovacs is a novel-in-verse Award-Winning Author whose love for poetry expands across his many profound stories. He is an avid cook who is passionate about fitness and dedicated to his family. He served in the Army Reserves for 13 years and is still currently serving in the Air National Guard.

Stan Lake is a writer, photographer, and filmmaker from Bethania, North Carolina. He enlisted in the NC Army National Guard as a 13M in 2001 and later deployed to support Operation Iraqi Freedom from 2005 to 2006 with A 5-113th FAR doing convoy operations. For more info visit stanlakecreates.com

Jason Landau served 6 years in the Marines as a rifleman in Golf Company 2/25 out of Picatinny Arsenal NJ. From 2018-2019 I deployed to Helmand Province Afghanistan. During this time, he served as a Designated Marksman for his Platoon on an Afghan Police compound known as Bost, near Lashkar Gah.

Joshuah Landspurg is a former USAF TACP JTAC that deployed to Afghanistan with the 173rd Airborne in 2005 and Iraq with the 2nd BDE, 101st Airborne in 2007. He is currently a firefighter/paramedic in the city of Phoenix and a graduate writing student at Harvard Extension. When not working 24-hour shifts and spending time with the family, hobbies include writing, reading, jiu-jitsu (brown belt), gardening, and diving.

Martyn Lees, AKA Marty Le Renard, is a British veteran who, after 13 years deployed in Iraq, Afghanistan, Libya, and elsewhere, first as a paratrooper and later as a security contractor, has found peace with his wife on the Northern California coast, where he writes poetry inspired by his experiences at war, both for his country, and with himself.

Zach Lewis is an EOD Tech in the Marines. He is a father to a beautiful girl named Flora, and is a husband to a supportive wife. His joys include showing people how to tell authentic depression era glassware apart from reproductions, breakfast from Family Mart, and holding his daughter while dancing to The Cure.

Chris Madsen served as a Sniper with the 101st Airborne and deployed to Southwest Baghdad in 2005. His experiences there, along with the bonds formed within the platoon, served as motivation to live life with intention and purpose. After a significant life event in 2020 Chris found writing as a means for relief.

Adam Magers served in the US Army as a combat medic and "IED (Improvised Explosive Device) Hunter" in Baghdad during the Iraq War. Today he works as a psychotherapist and as the Clinical Manager at The Battle Within, a non-profit that provides quality therapeutic programs to veterans and first responders; in addition to serving clients at his private practice.

Don Mateer spends his time writing prose and poetry. When he is not writing he spends his time working, photography, hiking, and cycling in Oregon. While serving in the U.S. Army he deployed to Afghanistan.

Charles McCaffrey is a Navy Veteran; and an avid storyteller and writer. His work is greatly influenced by his time in the military; and reflects images and impressions of the places he visited and the experiences he had during his travels.

Andrew McFarland is a husband, father, firefighter, and veteran. He has been a DoA civilian firefighter at Fort McCoy, WI for over 7 years. Currently working on his Masters of Natural Resources at UWSP. In a previous life, he was a Paratrooper and an Infantryman with the 1-501st, Fort Richardson, Alaska. He deployed in support of Operation Enduring Freedom to Afghanistan in 11-12.

GySgt **Chase McGrorty-Hunter** currently facilitates the Career School SNCO Academy Quantico where he teaches warfighting philosophy, Maneuver Warfare, and wargaming. He is the founder of the Bayonet Warfighting Society on Instagram. His writings have been featured in Leatherneck Magazine, the Gazette, Lethal Minds Journal, as well as co-authoring *Destination Unknown Volume 4* published by Marine Corps University Press.

Stephen Medrano served for 7 years in the military. He has been married for 18 years to his beautiful wife, Dr. Sarah M. Medrano. He is a father to Connor, Madisyn Jane, Ella, and Colbie, two Great Danes, Jocko and Augie, and a cat named Cat. He is a UTSA graduate, medical sales rep, writer, and is pursuing an MBA from Texas A&M University.

J.R. Miller is originally from the great state of North Carolina and now resides in Anchorage, Alaska. The author of *A Hummingbird a Cigarette and a Sunrise*, he is currently serving as an infantryman with the 11th Airborne. He has hopes of making his parents proud, being a present father, and catching more waves than he misses.

Michael Moriarty served four years in the USMC as a Scout Sniper with STA 2/8, participated in Operation Provide Comfort, Northern Iraq. Twenty years later did a short two year hitch with USNR Coastal Riverine Squadron 8 as a Damage Controlmen / Tactical Boat Crewmen. Currently an Assistant Fire Chief.

Phillip Mullen is a NYC based writer you have never heard about, mostly because he never shares anything with anyone. Having served in Africa with New York's own Fighting Irish Infantry, he now spends most of his time looking for a good bar. When not scribbling occasional word combos, Phill hangs out with other writers who encourage each other's bad behavior.

Allan Cris Nunag, a U.S. Army Veteran, now a Community Outreach Specialist at U.S.VETS-Las Vegas a nonprofit that assists Veterans in Crisis. Through his military experience & empathetic nature, his writing reflects the resilience & unity of veterans, offering solace & inspiration to other wayward souls navigating similar journeys.

JP is an active duty Army officer serving at Fort Liberty, NC. He has always strived to use his talents and passions to support people and warfighting.

Kyle Phillips is currently a Firefighter/Paramedic. He occasionally writes and reads poetry. He served one tour in Afghanistan as an 11C. And he is still figuring life out.

Chris Pimentel was an 03 in the Anbar for OIF 2/3. He is from Kansas and lives in California.

Jake Pique joined the army as an infantryman when he was 17, and deployed to Nangarhar province, Afghanistan shortly after basic training. Spending his 18th birthday overseas he grew up fast, and he grew up hateful. Now that he's out of the military, he spends his time focusing on love and healing, primarily through writing and following Buddhist teachings.

Keavy Rake is an active-duty Air Force officer, she deployed once in support of Operation Inherent Resolve, and three times to Afghanistan with Special Operations. She was the last Air Force PAO in Afghanistan and the lead cultural liaison for 35,000 Afghans during Operation Allies Refuge at Ramstein AB, Germany. She is a wife, and mother to two grown sons

Mason Rodrigue grew up in heavily Catholic rural Louisiana. After an uninspiring college athletic career, he enlisted into the Marine Corps at 26, which is the basis of his award-winning debut poetry collection *Rock Eater*, in which he sets the record for most possible combinations of rhymes including the word "infantry."

Matthew Sabedra was born and raised in Central Texas and enlisted in the U.S. Army immediately after High School. After serving seven years as an All-Source Intelligence Analyst, Matthew attended the University of Colorado-Denver, where he received a Bachelor's in Anthropology.

Julian P. Seddon is a 35-year-old U.S. Marine veteran from Philadelphia, PA. He graduated with a BFA in creative writing from UNC Wilmington in May of 2021. One day he soon plans to publish a collection of war-poems. He also plans to one day to become unstuck in time.

Amy Sexauer is a poet that grew up traveling the world. After being raised in a military family, she spent nine years on active duty and is now serving in the U.S. Army Reserves. She is currently attending graduate school in Cambridge, Massachusetts where she lives with her daughter and two dogs.

Christian Sonnier served in the Army from 2004-2008 as a forward observer for the 3rd Ranger Battalion and the 82nd Airborne. He saw Iraq twice and Afghanistan once. He used his benefits to obtain a bachelor's in political science and a master's in public administration. He resides in Fort Worth, Texas.

DJ Sorensen was medically discharged due to a back injury back in 2016 leaving him angry as he tried to find his identity post-Army. A previously published poem in DRC's *War...&After*, encouraged him to continue writing.

SquidXIII is a multidimensional artist. He doesn't just create one type of work. Instead, his output spans both the written and visual arts. His portfolio is a testament to his human experience, and much of the work he makes is meant to engage with that experience on a deeper level.

Jacob Szydzik is a Father, Husband, Marine Corps Veteran. Over 8 years in the infantry allowed him to see the world in faithful service to our nation. He currently serves his community, raising a family and hopefully leaving something behind worthwhile before he shuffles off this mortal coil.

Depending on who is in the room, **Caleb Taylor** is either a salt dog or the bootest of boots. He thinks the truth is probably somewhere in the middle but definitely leaning towards boot.

Alex Tirabasso medically retired in July 2023 as a Special Forces Weapons Sergeant after 13 years in the Army. He lives in Colorado and is working on his Masters in Data Analytics.

Ali Watts is an OIF army veteran trying to put life into words and seeing if that makes sense to anyone else along the way. She's got a disproportionate kinship with satire, tugboats, and underdogs, and will listen to war stories until the sun comes up.

Evan Young Weaver is a New Hampshire native who aspires to be a better poet than he was a warrior. He prefers to write about love, and New England, and good dogs.

Luke Wood, an Air Force veteran, channels his military experiences into poignant poetry. Through his writing, he illuminates the stark realities of military service, exploring themes of disillusionment, sacrifice, and resilience. With raw emotion and vivid imagery, Wood invites readers to confront the complexities of war and its impact on the human spirit.

Billy Whitworth served in the Army for 15 years until 24 Feb 2024 and have one tour overseas supporting Operation Inherent Resolve. He has been writing songs, short stories, and poetry for 24 years.

PREVIOUSLY PUBLISHED WORKS BY DEAD RECKONING COLLECTIVE:

FACT & MEMORY by: Tyler Carroll & Keith Dow
IN LOVE… &WAR: THE POET WARRIOR ANTHOLOGY VOL. 1
WAR… &AFTER: THE POET WARRIOR ANTHOLOGY VOL. 2
WAR{N}PIECES by: Leo Jenkins
LUCKY JOE by: Brian Kimber, Leo Jenkins, and David Rose
SOBER MAN'S THOUGHTS by: William Bolyard
KARMIC PURGATORY by: Keith Dow
WAR IS A RACKET by: Smedley Butler
THE FIRST MARAUDER by: Luke Ryan
WHERE THEY MEET by: Cokie
POPPIES by: Amy Sexauer
ROCK EATER by: Mason Rodrigue
REVISION OF A MAN by: Matt Smythe
ON ASSIMILATION by: Leo Jenkins
SANGIN, THEN AND NOW by Neville Johnson
A WORD LIKE GOD by Leo Jenkins
PHANTOMS by Ben Fortier
KILLERS IN THEIR YOUTH by Nicholas Efstathiou
DOUBLE KNOT by Mac Caltrider
DEMONS IN THE TAILLIGHTS by William Bolyard
ODYSSEUS AND THE OAR by Adam Magers
SCREAMING EAGLES WINGS by David Rose
THE TRANSCRIPT by Nick Orton
SOMETIMES I GO AWAY by Steven M Callahan

DEAD RECKONING COLLECTIVE is a veteran owned and operated publishing company. Our mission encourages literacy as a component of a positive lifestyle. Although DRC only publishes the written work of military veterans, the intention of closing the divide between civilians and veterans is held in the highest regard. By sharing these stories it is our hope that we can help to clarify how veterans should be viewed by the public and how veterans should view themselves.

Visit us at:
deadreckoningco.com

@deadreckoningcollective

@deadreckoningco

@DRCpublishing

www.ingramcontent.com/pod-product-compliance
Lightning Source LLC
Chambersburg PA
CBHW071117160426
43196CB00013B/2608